Augustine Francis Hewit

The Teaching of St. John

The Apostle to the Churches of Asia and the World

Augustine Francis Hewit

The Teaching of St. John
The Apostle to the Churches of Asia and the World

ISBN/EAN: 9783337319427

Printed in Europe, USA, Canada, Australia, Japan

Cover: Foto ©Lupo / pixelio.de

More available books at **www.hansebooks.com**

THE TEACHING

OF

ST. JOHN THE APOSTLE

TO THE

Churches of Asia and the World

BY

AUGUSTINE FRANCIS HEWIT, D.D.
Of the Congregation of St. Paul.

NEW YORK
THE CATHOLIC BOOK EXCHANGE
120 West 60th Street
1895

CONTENTS.

	PAGE
THE TEACHING OF ST. JOHN THE APOSTLE,	1
ENCYCLICAL LETTER TO THE BISHOPS AND CHURCHES OF ASIA MINOR,	34
THE HOLY GOSPEL OF JESUS CHRIST, ACCORDING TO ST. JOHN,	47
AN EPISTLE OF ST. JOHN THE APOSTLE TO THE SEVEN CHURCHES OF ASIA,	149
INTRODUCTORY EPISTLE,	152
MESSAGE TO THE BISHOP OF EPHESUS,	155
MESSAGE TO THE BISHOP OF SMYRNA,	156
MESSAGE TO THE BISHOP OF PERGAMUS,	157
MESSAGE TO THE BISHOP OF THYATIRA,	158
MESSAGE TO THE BISHOP OF SARDIS,	160
MESSAGE TO THE BISHOP OF PHILADELPHIA,	161
MESSAGE TO THE BISHOP OF LAODICEA,	162

Nil Obstat:
>CAROLUS P. GRANNAN, S.T.D.,
>>*Censor Deputatus.*

Imprimatur:
>MICHAEL AUGUSTINUS,
>>*Archiepiscopus Neo-Eboracensis.*

Hail, full of grace, the Lord is with thee.—*St. Luke i. 28.*

In the beginning was the Word, and the Word was with God, and the Word was God.—St. John i. 1.

Mary went into the hill country and saluted Elizabeth.—*St. Luke i. 39, 40.*

THE TEACHING

OF

ST. JOHN THE APOSTLE.

THE object of the present little work is twofold. First, to present the evidence of the apostolic origin of the Catholic Church, with the dogma, hierarchy, and liturgy, from the inspired writings of St. John, and from the tradition received from him by his disciples and their immediate successors. Second, to offer a specimen of an improved English version of the sacred canonical Scriptures.

St. John fills an unique and most important position in the Primitive Christian Church. He survived his fellow-apostles, during a third of a century, having lived to near the age of one hundred years, and to near the close of the first century. He is the connecting link between the Apostles and the Bishops to whom they handed over the governing and teaching authority which they themselves had received immediately from Jesus Christ. In his person, and through him, the apostolic college bequeathed their blessing and sanction to the Catholic Episcopate and Church of the second century; its doctrines, rites, government, and entire constitution. They left also an anathema upon the rising heresies which disturbed the peace of the first age, and which inaugurated the anti-Apostolic, anti-Catholic, anti-Christian succession of false teachers, with their perverse doctrines and rebellious opposition to legitimate authority; that has kept up a continuous warfare against genuine Christianity through all ages down to the present day. The Orthodox and Catholic Christianity of the second, third, and fourth centuries shows itself with an ever-increasing and brightening light, from Clement, Ignatius, Polycarp, Irenæus, Victor, Cyprian; to Sylvester, Athanasius, the Cyrils, Basil, and the Gregories of Nyssa and Nazianzus. By tracing it to St. John, we prove that Nicene Christianity is apostolic in creed, worship, and order; having its authority and origin from Jesus Christ Himself, the Prophet, Priest, and King of the

Kingdom of Heaven on the earth. Nicene, Tridentine, and Vatican Christianity are identical. Therefore, the Catholic Hierarchy of this day clasps the hand of St. John, on whose head rested the hand of our Lord Jesus Christ; transmitting the electric current of truth and power to our own bishops and our sovereign pontiff, from whom we receive the light and grace of Christianity. We are in the most immediate contact with St. John, because he is the last of the apostles, and completed the New Testament, as Evangelist and Prophet, by his Gospel, Epistles, and Apocalypse, giving us the last words of inspiration, and closing the book of divine revelation.

St. John possessed plenary apostolic authority, given him directly by Jesus Christ; and, of course, he could exercise his apostolic commission anywhere in the world, and at any time during his life, like the other apostles; although in subordination to the supreme authority of St. Peter, and in accordance with laws which may have been enacted by the apostolic college, or with mutual agreements which any of them may have entered into among themselves, as to a division of missionary districts. St. John confined himself during the last thirty years of his life to Asia Minor, where, St. Jerome tells us, he founded and governed all the churches: "*Totas Asiæ ecclesias fundavit ac rexit.*" This means, of course, that the churches not previously founded by St. Paul and others were founded by him or under his direction, and that he governed them all by his supreme apostolic authority. He established sees, and consecrated bishops, among others St. Polycarp of Smyrna, his favorite disciple. His chief residence was Ephesus, although he did not make that or any other city his episcopal see. As apostle, he was superior to all bishops, but in a manner more like the supervision of a Papal Legate than that of an ordinary Primate.

The doctrine preached, and the order established by St. John, during the closing period of the first century, are the model on which Eastern Catholicism was formed, and also the Church of France. This is not

And seeing, they understood of the word that had been spoken of them by the shepherds.—*St. Luke* ii. 17.

intended to be a statement that this model of Catholic organization was first established in Ephesus and the neighboring episcopal sees, and afterwards copied by other churches. Jerusalem, Antioch, Rome, and Alexandria, as well as other apostolic sees, were equally models in doctrine and order. But in Ephesus we perceive very distinctly what the apostolic model was, which was the same everywhere, and from one specimen we learn the characteristics of all.

That episode of ecclesiastical history, the administration of St. John in Asia, of which we obtain glimpses, would have a wonderful charm, if complete biographies of the Apostle, of St. Timothy, of St. Polycarp, of their companions and disciples, together with the annals of their missions, of the churches they founded, the persecutions they endured, and descriptions of their liturgical rites, their social life, pictures of all the scenes of this new Christianity arising amid the fanes, theatres, and market-places of heathenism, had been carefully recorded and handed down to us. We may lament, but cannot supply the loss, except by an imperfect effort of the imagination to amplify the hints, and fill out the faint lines of early and scanty Christian literature.

The thirty years of the inchoate, provisional, and missionary operations and arrangements of the apostles and apostolic men, who were the founders of Christianity, had passed away; and with an incredible rapidity and solidity the splendid edifice of the Church had arisen throughout and beyond the bounds of the Roman Empire. The apostles and the first generation of Christians had passed away, with the exception of St. John and a few other survivors. Bishops had succeeded to the apostles, and Popes to their prince. Although the origin of that elaborate hierarchical order, and the division of the universal Church into patriarchates, exarchates, provinces, and dioceses, with an organized clergy under bishops; an order corresponding to the political divisions of the empire; cannot be traced with historical accuracy, yet its beginnings appear already early in the second century. The names by which all these ecclesiastical distinctions were known at a later period do not, indeed, appear in a fixed and definite sense, at first; but the things which they designate show themselves with a gradually increasing precision during the two centuries immediately succeeding the apostolic age; and even, in a certain measure, both the things and their names are to be found, even during the first century, and in the books of the sacred canon.

Notwithstanding the veil which the Discipline of the Secret threw over the most sacred mysteries of religion, the creed and dogmatic teaching of the Church begins to show more clearly its symmetrical form and divinely beautiful features. The heresies which began so soon to pervert and counterfeit the genuine gospel, acted as a foil to the truth, and gave occasion to more definite statements and a more stringent discipline.

But I must confine myself to the apostolic teaching and administration of St. John, and not make excursions into other regions of the ecclesiastical domain.

Those who have assailed Catholic dogma, have at times denied the genuineness of the writings of St. John, chiefly because of their distinctly Catholic, dogmatic character. Critical discussions have made this position untenable. The doctrine and discipline of St. John as an apostle stand out in unmistakable historical lines. His doctrine is Catholic dogma, his discipline is Catholic hierarchical order. Those who assert that this dogmatic and hierarchical Catholicism was an innovation on the pure Gospel of Christ, must maintain either that St. John was one of the principal innovators, or that the change was made by others, without his participation. This is their dilemma. If others planned and began the alteration of the Christian Gospel, without his participation, it is inconceivable that he should not have perceived and denounced this conspiracy, as he did denounce the heresies of the Gnostics, and give warning of the coming of Antichrist. On the other hand, it is inconceivable that the beloved disciple of Jesus, the guardian and protector of his blessed Mother, the eagle of the Gospel, should have been an innovator, either by a blundering misunderstanding of his Master's character and teaching, or by a wilful usurpation of the office of founding a religion and a church. St. John's Gospel is the true and genuine Gospel of Jesus Christ. It is identical with the gospel of the first three centuries of the Catholic Church. And this is enough to make it evident that the Nicene, Catholic Christianity is the original, authentic Christianity of Christ. The one point of vital importance is, to show the identity of the Catholicism of the second, third, and fourth centuries, in its dogmatic and hierarchical elements, with the apostolic teaching and discipline of St. John.

There is a Newest Gospel, whose disciples call themselves by the honorable name of "Evangelical," which is in equal opposition to the Old Gospel of Catholic Orthodoxy, and the New Gospel, which we call, by courtesy, Protestant Orthodoxy. Dr. Harnack is the Luther of this Newest Gospel, which he proclaims with a learning, ability, and we are fain to admit with a religious earnestness, which entitle him to the respect even of his most decided opponents.

This Newest Gospel is substantially a religion of Theism, practical as well as theoretical, which proclaims that God is properly called Father, as being the Father of men, whom he invites to a spiritual sonship. Jesus Christ, who is a pure man, is the Son of God, *par excellence*, by reason of his perfect and ideal holiness, and an exaltation to the place and office of the Lord of his human brethren. The Apostles' Creed with all its developments, the whole dogmatic system founded upon it, together with the teaching authority, the sacerdotal order, and the efficacious sacraments of the Church, are rejected as human inventions.

Professor Harnack has done great service by bringing the controversy respecting the true and genuine nature of Christianity to a simple and intelligible issue within confined limits. He has shown at what an early period Catholicism was universally prevalent; and that it is implied in the accep-

They presented unto Him gifts; gold, and frankincense, and myrrh.
—*St. Matthew ii. 11.*

tance of the Creed and the Bible as final, authoritative rules of faith. In short, the controversy is reduced to the question, whether the eternal Son of God was made man, redeemed the world by dying, rose again bodily from the grave, and left a law of faith and obedience to the apostles, to be proclaimed to all mankind as the way of salvation.

This question is sufficiently and easily determined by a simple and clear exposition of the Apostolic Teaching of St. John.

In the first place, the dogma of the true and proper divinity of Jesus Christ, which includes the dogma of the Trinity of Persons in the Godhead, is most clearly affirmed and taught by the Apostle. It is only necessary to read his Gospel and the Epistle which is an introduction to it, in order to be convinced of this. This twofold dogma is the very substance of the Creed, in the simpler form which is called the Symbol of the Apostles, in the more expanded and definite Symbol adopted by the Councils of Nicæa, Constantinople, Lyons, and Florence; in the Creed called by the name of St. Athanasius, and in the Creed of Pope Pius IV. It is the subject-matter of the definitions of the first six councils.

There is at present an active and earnest controversy going on in Germany respecting the origin, history, and authority of the Symbol of the Apostles. It is of secondary importance to determine the origin of the *verbal formula*. The essential thing is to show that the dogmas commonly called the twelve articles of faith, especially the mysteries of the Trinity and the Incarnation, and moreover all the doctrines of the Catholic faith implicitly or virtually contained in the Creed, are of apostolic origin, received by the apostles through the revelation of Jesus Christ. If this be not so, the cause of Christianity is lost. For some minds of the nobler sort, a philosophical and even a religious Theism may remain; and a great reverence may be cherished for the persons of Jesus Christ, his apostles, and their illustrious successors. But we cannot consent to call this Christianity; and it is no more, in substance, than the profession of some advocates of an eclectic and comprehensive world-religion who do not call themselves Christians. Some distinction must be made, however, in favor of those who, although pure humanitarians, admit that Jesus Christ has been made, in some true sense, the Lord of this world.

The Catholic contention is for the true and proper Divinity of the Eternal Son of the Eternal Father, two distinct Persons subsisting with the Third Person, the Holy Spirit proceeding from the Father and the Son, in One Divine Essence. And for the true Incarnation of the Son of God by his conception and birth of the Virgin Mother, through the quickening agency of the Holy Spirit.

St. John wrote his Gospel at the solicitation of the bishops of Asia Minor, not exclusively but yet primarily in order to set forth the Catholic doctrine of the Incarnation, in opposition to the heresies of Cerinthus, Ebion, and the earliest Gnostics. His First Epistle is an Encyclical addressed to these bishops, as an introduction to the Gospel.

It would be superfluous to make an exposition of the Christology of St. John, since by far the shortest and most satisfactory way of understanding it, is just to read his text, without note or comment.

St. John emphatically declares that the doctrine which he preaches is the revealed truth of God, the faith which must be believed in order to be saved, and that every contrary teaching is deadly heresy. This faith was committed to the apostles, from whom the faithful have received it, and are in the communion of the Church; which, if a real and perfect communion, is a fellowship with the Father and the Son in the Spirit. This tradition is the proximate rule of faith, and a departure from it and secession from apostolic fellowship is the test and touchstone of heresy, and of the spirit of Antichrist. The subdued, smooth, and quiet manner in which the text runs along like a clear and tranquil stream, without emphasis of distinct passages, or logical construction of propositions and conclusions, makes it easy to pass over the surface without noticing the definite and profound ideas which an attentive consideration discloses. But, if one will read the First Epistle of St. John in the light of that clear view of its scope which is suggested and verified by a close examination of its sentences and words, he will see that there are several golden threads on which its detached pearls are strung and bound together into a connected chaplet.

In the first place, its scope is dogmatic, and makes a fit introduction to the dogmatic part of the Gospel. The Incarnation is presented as the primary and essential object of faith.

In the second place, this formal object which terminates the act of saving faith, is a truth of divine revelation committed to the apostles, and through the medium of this apostolic teaching communicated to the faithful.

In the third place, the faithful are united in one communion by their adhesion to the apostolic authority.

In the fourth place, this steadfastness in the unity of the apostolic communion is the condition of spiritual life, of fellowship with God in Christ, and of everlasting salvation.

It is enough to refer the reader to the text itself of the Epistle, without giving a running commentary by way of exposition. I will cite only one passage, pregnant with the whole Catholic doctrine of authority in the teaching of dogmatic truth, a passage admirably explained and applied in one of the earliest of the Oxford Tracts:

"*We* are of God. He that knoweth God, heareth *Us*. He that is not of God, heareth not *Us*. *By this we know the spirit of truth and the spirit of error*" (iv. 6).

The "We" are, first of all, the apostles. The Epistle begins with this pronoun, and designates by it unmistakably the apostles, who bear witness to that which St. John says: "*We* have seen and heard, and declare unto *you*, that *you* also may have fellowship with *Us*." Since the other apostles were long since dead; since the immediate governing and teaching authority was actually in the hands of the bishops; and the

Lord, now lettest thou thy servant depart in peace, according to the word. For mine eyes have seen thy salvation.—*St. Luke ii. 29, 30.*

bishops of Asia Minor were especially addressed in this Epistle, it is fair to infer that St. John includes the bishops along with himself, as the body whose teaching authority was the proximate rule of faith, and the touchstone of heresy. Wherefore, the sense of the passage is, that the Catholic Episcopate which was founded in the apostles has a divine authority which those who are taught of God obey; and by which the Catholic Church is rendered infallible in faith; so that the mark of truth is conformity to Catholic Doctrine, and the mark of error is non-conformity to the same. The faithful, by participation, share in the gifts primarily imparted to the apostles and their successors. The *Ecclesia Docens* and the *Ecclesia Discens* are one; there is an active and a passive infallibility; conformity to the doctrine of the Catholic Church, and submission to the authority of the Catholic Episcopate, are one and the same thing.

The Newest German Gospel can obtain no countenance from St. John. It must reject his authority in order to keep its footing. It seems, indeed, that he must have foreseen all the errors which it advocates, and that he intended to warn the faithful against these errors, as well as those of Cerinthus and the Ebionites, with which, indeed, they have a great similarity. If this Newest Gospel were truly the genuine, original Gospel of Christ, it would follow that Cerinthus was the apostolical and evangelical teacher, and St. John the innovator and heretic.

The Real Presence is another distinctive Catholic dogma most clearly taught by St. John, who in this teaching is merely the mouth-piece of the Lord himself, in the sixth chapter of his Gospel. The Real Presence, distinctly understood and explained, implies Transubstantiation and the Unbloody Sacrifice of the New Law, the Holy Eucharist. It implicitly includes the true and proper priesthood of the apostles and their successors of the first and second order, the bishops and presbyters who have received the indelible character of the Sacrament of Order.

Tradition adds to this express written testimony of the Gospel its witness to the origin of one of the principal ancient liturgies from St. John, by whose name it was called. The scenic representations of the Apocalypse, in which four-and-twenty elders surround the throne, and incense is offered before the altar, are totally out of harmony with the old and new evangelical ideal of the Church. The seven angels of the seven churches, which are often interpreted to represent all churches in every age and region of the world, or all the different phases of the Catholic Church, are so manifestly the bishops of those churches, that it is surprising any one should have questioned it. There is such a hierarchical and liturgical atmosphere about these churches of the exarchate of Ephesus, that certain writers have supposed that the transformation from Congregationalism to Episcopacy began in this region. Polycrates, Bishop of Ephesus during the latter part of the second century, mentions the fact that St. John wore a coronet of gold—*i. e.*, a crown-shaped mitre. This is a very significant incident, showing the sacerdotal character of the Christian ministry at its earliest period. The firmness of St. Polycarp and his fellow-bishops in adhering to the custom of celebrating Easter according to the day of the month, with the Jews, and not invariably on a Sunday; and the obstinacy of the bishops of the same exarchate under their primate Polycrates, in resisting the demand of Pope Victor that they should conform to the Roman custom; furnish a stringent proof of the ecclesiastical spirit which governed them. The question of the exact time of keeping Easter was one which regarded a ritual observance of minor importance. The keeping of Lent and Easter was a matter of great importance, and so also was uniformity of customs in respect to times. But, the Roman and Asiatic customs were each equally good and equally indifferent in themselves, apart from the advantages of uniformity, and the disadvantages of difference. Nevertheless, this minor ritual question was regarded as a matter of

He took the young child and his mother, and departed into Egypt.—
St. Matthew ii. 13.

ST. JOHN THE APOSTLE.

so much consequence in that early time, that it gave rise to vehement controversies in various parts of the Church. This is a proof that the Puritanical spirit of disregarding rites and ceremonies, and that which is called the evangelical simplicity of primitive Christianity, excluding sacerdotalism, liturgical forms, and the whole system of external Catholicism, have no existence even in the first two centuries. In fact, these early Christians carried their regard for these external ordinances to an extreme. The resistance of St. Polycarp and Polycrates to the wise and enlightened efforts of Popes Anicetus and Victor to establish uniformity of discipline and ritual, proves what an exaggerated deference they cherished for an ordinance of St. John in a non-essential matter. And this very fault of excessive ecclesiasticism shows how very ecclesiastical was the religious system and order established by St. John during the period of his apostolic administration.

Another thing, also, is proved by the tenacious adherence in this and other cases to every tradition which was, or was supposed to be, apostolic. This is, namely, the impossibility which would have met and overcome every attempt; even though supported by high ecclesiastical authority, or the very highest, that is the Roman See; to innovate in essential matters upon the doctrine and discipline of the apostles. The pretence of a radical change, a specific transformation, from a religion like that of old Puritanism or the new Prussian Evangelicalism, into Catholicism; between the latter part of the first and the end of the second century; is the most absurd and fanciful of hypotheses; deserving rather to be called a dream than an hypothesis. The Mohammedan legend, that Abraham grew in a week from infancy to manhood by sucking his two thumbs; and the Irish legend of the swans transformed into human beings and baptized by St. Patrick; are more credible than this myth, which great scholars are reduced to the necessity of vindicating. In the first legend, it was a human infant who attained only his natural development according to his specific type, by an accelerated process. The swans were really the princely children of Lir restored to their proper and natural shape. But the supposed transformation of Christianity is like the change of a young lamb into a stalwart youth, of an actual bird into a human being.

The dogma of the One Catholic Church is in the Gospel of St. John, not taught in his own words, but breathed forth in that sublime prayer offered by the Lord in the Cœnaculum, on the night of his betrayal and the eve of his crucifixion. That the communion of the apostles is the bond of this unity, we have seen that St. John teaches most distinctly. But, besides this, we can find in the teaching and history of St. John indications of that principle of unity in the apostolate by virtue of which it is made a bond of unity in the Catholic Church; the primacy of St. Peter which his successors in the Roman See inherited.

St. John is the only one of the evangelists who relates the circumstance of the change of the name of the chief apostle from Simon to Peter. This he does in the beginning of his Gospel, immediately after narrating the baptism of Jesus and his designation by John the Baptist as the Messiah.

"Andrew, the brother of Simon Peter, was one of the two who had heard from John and followed him. He findeth first his brother Simon, and saith to him: we have found the *Messiah*, which is, being interpreted, the *Christ*. And he brought him to Jesus. And Jesus looking upon him said: "Thou art Simon the son of Jona; *thou shalt be called Cephas, which is, being interpreted, Peter*" (i. 40-42). This suffices as a proof of the whole Catholic doctrine of the supremacy of the See of St. Peter. In the name *Christ* is involved the entire doctrine of the Incarnation, as developed, defined, and declared in Catholic Theology. After this divine Name which designates the Person of the Son of God made man and redeeming the world, comes the Name which designates the Person of the Head of the Church, through which Christ re-

And he was subject unto them.—*St. Luke ii. 51.*
And the child grew and waxed strong.—*St. Luke ii. 40.*

deems the world. This solemn and mysterious bestowal of the Name Peter, taken in connection with the other texts of the Gospels which explain its significance, is so plainly an appointment of St. Peter to the supreme headship of the Catholic Church, that nothing can be added to and nothing taken away from its evident purport. It is only the insensibility of the inward ear of the mind, caused by incessant repetition of the words in which the Gospel declares that St. Peter is the rock on which the Church is built, and by the incessant denial that they mean anything, which causes them to pass unheeded. To a simple, unbiassed mind which listens to them attentively, knowing what the Catholic Church teaches and what the Popes claim in regard to the supremacy of the Roman Church, they can convey no other sense than the Catholic sense. As a little child, I received this impression like the stamp of a seal on soft wax, and it has remained ineffaceable.

The history of St. John casts a peculiar and interesting sidelight on the primacy of

St. Peter and his successors, which is faint indeed, but in the absence of the direct and clear light which we would wish to have, is of great value. St. John is chiefly known to us as he became in his old age, the contemplative theologian and the apostle of love. In his youth, he was like the eagle, not so much by his high flights into the upper air of mystic contemplation, as by his soaring ambition to make his eyrie on lofty summits of dignity. There was not only a virginal purity but also a glowing fire in his character, and the brothers James and John were called "Sons of Thunder." They were evidently jealous of Peter, and induced their mother, whose example has since then been often imitated, to intercede with their Lord for the highest places in that coming kingdom which they imagined to be one of worldly splendor. The gentle reproofs of the Lord, and the sweet influence of the Blessed Mother bequeathed by her Son at death to his filial care; but above all the extraordinary gifts of the Holy Ghost sent down upon the apostles on the day of

Pentecost; elevated the character of the juvenile and impetuous disciple of Jesus to the sublime height of sanctity in which all his natural imperfections disappeared.

There is no more trace of ambition and the desire of pre-eminence visible in his conduct. As an apostle, he shared with St. Peter universal jurisdiction and authority. Yet there is no record of his exercising his apostolic office outside of Asia Minor, and after the death of St. Peter and the other apostles, although he may be said to have inherited as the sole survivor of the apostolic college all the prerogatives of their divine commission, except the primacy of Peter, there is no sign of his assuming any jurisdiction over the bishops in the Church at large.

All this falls in with the historical tradition that St. Peter's primacy had passed to his successors in the Roman See, of whom there were three who ruled during the last period of St. John's life; viz., Linus, Anacletus, and Clement. There is no record of the exercise of papal power by the first two of these Popes. There is an almost total dearth of historical information about these last decades of the first century. Moreover, there was no call for the personal, immediate intervention and direction of the Popes. The apostles were coadjutors of St. Peter in his universal primacy, in order that the work of founding the Church, for which one man was inadequate, might be accomplished by thirteen, aided by a sufficient number of missionaries. When this first great work had been accomplished and the apostles had departed this life, the primacy devolved on the successor of St. Peter in the Roman Chair, and the bishops succeeded only to the ordinary episcopal authority of the apostles. They were coadjutors of the universal bishop, within the limits of their dioceses but not in the government of the universal Church, unless specially called to his councils or as members of a universal synod. It was not necessary for St. Peter to go through the whole world founding and governing churches. He exercised his supreme

After three days they found him in the temple in the midst of the doctors.—*St. Luke ii. 46.*

power virtually through the other apostles. In like manner, in local and ordinary affairs, the Supreme Pontiff was virtually and sufficiently personated and represented by each bishop, and the Roman Church by provincial councils. The cases did not at once arise and become numerous, which called for the exercise of a higher and more universal authority, especially as long as persecution placed most serious obstacles in the way of inter-communion between distant churches.

Before the end of the first century, one case did arise of which the record has been preserved, that called for the interference of a supreme judge and ruler. It was the dissension between the clergy and people of Corinth. Immediately, recourse is had to Rome, as the capital city of the ecclesiastical kingdom, and to St. Clement, its bishop; and not to St. John, the surviving apostle, who was at Ephesus, much nearer to Corinth, and still in possession of his original apostolic authority. He is not appealed to, and he does not interfere. Within his

Asiatic Diocese he continues to exercise his apostolic primacy over bishops and churches, but not beyond this circle. Evidently, the administration of the Catholic Church having passed from the apostles to the bishops, and the primacy from the chief apostle to the chief bishop, the universal jurisdiction of St. John, though not formally withdrawn, was in practical abeyance; and in his restricted, local exercise of apostolic authority over bishops, he was, *de facto*, a legate of the Pope as successor to St. Peter in his supremacy, although he held his commission directly from Jesus Christ, and not from Clement.

Clement breaks the silence of the Apostolic See in his Epistle to the Corinthians, with a calm and quiet consciousness and assertion of authority, that awakens no protest from Corinth, and least of all from St. John, whose acquiescence is an indication that the supremacy of the Roman Church was universally recognized and indisputable. It is a remarkable fact, that the discovery of the passages which were wanting to a complete text of the Epistle, in which newly discovered passages are some of its strongest expressions of authority, is due to a Greek prelate, and its translation into English to an Anglican prelate. Its tone of authority is unmistakable. If the papal supremacy were really a usurpaticn, Clement in the first, and Victor in the second century, would have to be regarded as the precursors of the later Leos, Gregorys, and Innocents. In this case, it is incredible that St. John would not have raised his voice in remonstrance, as Tertullian did, a century later; incredible that the great Prophet of the New Law who foresaw and foretold the coming of Antichrist and all the great events of church-history from his own time to the end of the world, would not have given warning of the rise of that great power which was aiming at sovereignty in Christendom.

From St. Irenæus we gain a direct and satisfactory knowledge of the doctrine and polity of the churches under the immediate oversight of St. John. Polycarp was St. John's disciple, and was ordained by him

Bishop of Smyrna. Irenæus was the disciple of Polycarp, and was moreover intimately acquainted with the principal churches both of the East and the West. We learn from him what was the doctrine and the administration of the apostle, and that there was perfect unity and agreement among all the apostolic churches. The doctrine of St. Irenæus has been so often and so fully explained, that it is needless to say more on the topic in this place, except that it is Catholicism pure and simple.

This may suffice by way of introduction to the sublime, inspired text of St. John. I have not made a new version, and have made as few changes as possible in that old English version which has come down from the Catholic ages of England, and is substantially the same in those English Bibles which have been in common use during the past three centuries, with some variations of more or less importance in the different versions. The sense and meaning of all that part of St. John's writings which is contained in this volume is plain enough; and

He went up into a mountain. His disciples came to him. And opening his mouth he taught them.—*St. Matthew v. 2.*

I have followed the guidance of that rule which the Council of Trent prescribes, viz.: the Latin Vulgate. So far as accuracy is concerned, Archbishop Kenrick's revision of the Douay and Rheims version furnishes the Catholic reader with all that he could desire in an English Bible. What is still to be desired, is a correct version in *good English* of the antique pattern. I have tried the experiment in the present volume of furnishing a specimen of such a version, in the Gospel of St. John. I hope it may awaken attention to an acknowledged want, and suggest to our bishops the importance of taking efficient measures to supply it. I will add, also, the remark: that all those portions of holy Scripture which are contained in the Marquess of Bute's English Breviary, come up so close to the desirable standard, in my opinion, that a similar version of the whole Bible would be precisely what is wanted for the common use of our Catholic laity.

Feast of St. Thomas Aquinas.

ENCYCLICAL LETTER
OF
ST. JOHN THE APOSTLE TO THE BISHOPS AND CHURCHES OF ASIA MINOR.

THAT which was from the beginning, which We have heard, which We have seen with our eyes, which We have looked upon and our hands have handled, concerning the Word of Life; (and the Life was manifested, and We have seen and bear witness, and declare unto you the Eternal Life which was with the Father, and hath appeared unto Us), that which We have seen and heard declare We unto you, that ye also may have fellowship with Us; and that our common fellowship may be with the Father, and with his Son Jesus Christ. And these things write We unto you, that ye may rejoice, yea, that your joy may be full. This, then, is the message which We have heard from him and declare unto you: That God is light, and in him is no darkness at all. If we say that we have fellowship with him and walk in darkness, we lie, and do not the truth. But if we walk in the light, as he also is in the light, we have fellowship with one another, and the blood of Jesus Christ his Son cleanseth us from all sin. If we say that we have no sin, we deceive ourselves, and the truth is not in us. If we confess our sins, he is faithful and just, to forgive us our sins, and to cleanse us from all unrighteousness. If we say that we have not sinned, we make him a liar, and his word is not in us.

My little children, I write these things to you, that ye sin not. But, if any one hath sinned, we have an advocate with the Father, Jesus Christ the Righteous. And he is the propitiation for our sins; not, indeed, for ours only, but also for those of the whole world. And hereby do we know that we have known him, if we keep his commandments. Whoever saith that he hath known him and doth not keep his commandments is a liar, and the truth is not in him. But whoever keepeth his word, truly the love of God in him is perfect, and by this we know that we are in him. He who saith that he abideth in him, ought himself also to walk, even as he walked. Dearly beloved, I write no new commandment unto you, but an old commandment which ye had from the beginning. The old commandment is the word which ye have heard. Again, a new commandment I write unto you, which thing is true in him and in you; because the darkness is past, and the true light now shineth. He who saith that he is in the light, and hateth his brother, is in darkness, even until now. He that loveth his brother abideth in the light, and there is no occasion of stumbling in him. But he who hateth his brother is in darkness, and walketh in darkness, and knoweth not whither he goeth, because darkness hath blinded his eyes. I write unto you, my little children, because your sins are forgiven you for his name's sake. I write unto you, fathers, because ye have known him who is from the beginning. I write unto you, young men, because ye have overcome

Jesus saith unto her, Give me to drink.—*St. John iv. 7.*

the wicked one. I write unto you, children, because ye have known the Father. I write unto you, young men, because ye are strong, and the word of God abideth in you, and ye have overcome the wicked one. Love not the world, nor the things that are in the world. If any one love the world, the love of the Father is not in him. For all that is in the world is the lust of the flesh, and the lust of the eyes, and the pride of life, which is not of the Father, but is of the world. And the world passeth away, and the lust thereof; but he who doeth the will of God abideth for ever. Little children, it is the last hour, and as ye have heard that the Antichrist cometh, even already many Antichrists have arisen; whence we know that it is the last hour. They went out from us, but they were not of us; for if they had been of us, they would doubtless have remained with us; but they went out, that they might show plainly that they are not all of us. But ye have an anointing from the Holy One; and have known all things. I have not written to you as to those who know not the truth, but as to those who know it, and that no lie is of the truth. Who is the liar, but he who denieth that Jesus is the Christ. This is the Antichrist, who denieth the Father and the Son. Whosoever denieth the Son, neither hath he the Father; whosoever confesseth the Son, hath also the Father. As for you; let that which ye have from the beginning abide in you; if that which ye have heard from the beginning abide in you, ye also shall abide in the Son, and in the Father. And this is the promise which he hath promised to us, the life which is eternal. These things have I written unto you concerning those who would lead you astray. And as for you, let the anointing ye have received from him abide in you. And ye have no need that any one teach you, but as his anointing teacheth you of all things, it is in very deed true, and is no falsehood. And as he hath taught you, abide in him. And now, my little children, abide in him, that, when he shall appear we may have confidence, and not be made ashamed before him, at his coming. If ye know that he is righteous, know also that every one who doeth righteousness is born of him.

Behold, what manner of love the Father hath bestowed on us, that we should be called, and should be the sons of God; therefore, the world hath not known us, because it hath not known him. Dearly beloved, now are we the sons of God, and it doth not yet appear what we shall be. But we know that when he shall appear, we shall be like him, for we shall see him as he is. And every one who hath this hope sanctifieth himself even as he is holy. Every one who committeth sin, committeth also a transgression of the law; and sin is a transgression of the law. And ye know that he hath appeared that he might take away our sins; and in him is no sin. Every one who abideth in him sinneth not; and whosoever sinneth, hath not seen him, nor known him. My little children, let no one lead you astray. Whosoever worketh righteousness is righteous, as he also is righteous. Whosoever committeth sin is of the devil, for the devil sinneth from the beginning. For this end hath the Son of God appeared, that he may destroy the works of the devil. Whosoever hath been born of God doth not commit sin, because his seed remaineth in him, and he cannot sin because he hath been born of God. In this the children of God are manifest, and the children of the devil. Whosoever is not righteous, is not of God, neither he who loveth not his brother; for this is the message which ye have heard from the beginning, that ye love one another. Not as Cain, who was of the wicked one, and who killed his brother. And wherefore did he kill him? Because his own works were evil, and his brother's righteous. Marvel not, my brethren, if the world hate you. We know that we have passed out of death into life, because we love the brethren. He who loveth not, remaineth in death. Whosoever hateth his brother is a murderer, and ye know that no murderer hath eternal life abiding in him. By this we have known

Behold the sepulchre and how his body was laid.—*St. Luke xxiii. 55.*

the love of God, because he laid down his life for us; wherefore we ought to lay down our lives for the brethren. Whosoever hath the substance of this world, and seeth his brother having need, and shutteth up his compassion from him; how can the love of God abide in him? My little children, let us not love in word, only, and with the tongue, but in deed and in truth. By this we know that we are in the truth, and hereby shall we assure our hearts in his sight. For, if our heart reproach us, God is greater than our heart and knoweth all things. Dearly beloved, if our heart reproach us not, we have confidence towards God; and whatsoever we shall ask we shall receive from him, because we keep his commandments, and do the things which are pleasing in his sight. Moreover, this is his commandment; that we believe in the name of his Son, Jesus Christ, and love one another, as he hath given us commandment. Now, whosoever keepeth his commandment abideth in him, and hath him also abiding in himself, and hereby we know that he abideth in us, to wit, from the Spirit whom he hath given us.

Dearly beloved, believe not every spirit, but try the spirits, whether they be of God, because many false prophets are gone out into the world. Hereby is known the spirit which is of God. Every spirit that confesseth that Jesus Christ has come in the flesh, is from God; and every spirit that dissolveth Jesus, is not from God. And this is Antichrist, of whom ye have heard that he cometh, and who, indeed, is already in the world. Ye are of God, my little children, and ye have overcome him, because greater is he who is in you, than he who is in the world. They are of the world, therefore speak they of the world, and the world heareth them. We are of God. He that hath known God heareth Us, he that is not of God heareth not Us. Hereby know we the spirit of truth and the spirit of error. Dearly beloved, let us love one another, for love is from God. And every one who loveth hath been born of God, and knoweth God. Whosoever loveth not, hath not known God; for God is love. Hereby hath the love of God been manifested in us, inasmuch as God hath sent his Only-Begotten Son into the world that we may live through him. Herein is love, not as if we had loved God, but that he first loved us, and sent his Son, a propitiation for our sins. Dearly beloved, if God so loved us, we also ought to love one another. No man hath seen God at any time. If we love one another, God abideth in us, and his love is made perfect in us. Hereby we know that we abide in him, and he is in us, because he hath given us of his Spirit. And We have seen and bear witness, that God hath sent his Son to be the Saviour of the world. Whosoever shall confess that Jesus is the Son of God, God abideth in him, and he in God. And we have known, and have believed in the love which God hath toward us. God is Love; and he who abideth in love abideth in God, and God in him. Herein is the love of God made perfect with us, that we may have confidence in the day of judgment, because as he is, so are we also in this world. There is no fear in love, but perfect love casteth out fear; because fear hath torment. Wherefore he who feareth is not made perfect in love. Let us therefore love God, because God hath first loved us. If any one say, I love God; and hate his brother; he is a liar. For he who loveth not his brother whom he seeth, how can he love God whom he doth not see? And this commandment we have from God, that he who loveth God, love also his brother.

Whosoever believeth that Jesus is the Christ hath been born of God. And whosoever loveth him, loveth also him who hath been born of him. Hereby we know that we love the children of God, when we love God and keep his commandments. For this is the love of God, that we keep his commandments; and his commandments are not grievous. For whatsoever is born of God overcometh the world; and this is the victory that overcometh the world, even our faith. Who is he that overcometh the world, but he who believeth that Jesus is

There were brought unto him little children, that he should put his hands on them.—*St. Matthew xix. 13.*

the Son of God? This is he who came by water and blood, Jesus Christ; not by water only, but by water and blood. And it is the Spirit that beareth witness, because the Spirit is the Truth. For there are three who bear witness in heaven, the Father, and the Word, and the Holy Ghost; and the three are one. And there are three that bear witness on the earth, the spirit, and the water, and the blood, and these three are one. If we receive the witness of men, the witness of God is greater, for this is that witness of God which is greater, that God hath borne witness of his Son. And this is the witness, that God hath given to us life eternal, and this life is in his Son. Whosoever hath the Son hath the life; and whosoever hath not the Son, hath not the life. These things have I written to you, that ye may know that ye have eternal life, who believe in the name of the Son of God. And this is the confidence which we have towards him; that whatsoever we ask according to his will, he heareth us. Whatsoever we ask; we know that we have the requests which we ask of him. Whoever knoweth his brother to sin a sin not unto death, let him pray, and life shall be given to him who sinneth not unto death. There is sin unto death, for this I say not that any one should ask. All unrighteousness is sin; and there is sin unto death. We know that every one who hath been born of God, sinneth not; but that which was begotten of God keepeth him, and the Evil One toucheth him not. We know that we are of God, and the whole world lieth under the Evil One. And we know that the Son of God hath come, and hath given us understanding, that we may know the true God, and may be in his true Son. He is the true God and the life eternal.

My little children, keep yourselves from idols. Amen.

THE HOLY GOSPEL
OF
JESUS CHRIST, ACCORDING TO ST. JOHN.

In the beginning was the Word, and the Word was with God, and the Word was God. The same was in the beginning with God. All things were made through him, and without him was not anything made that was made. In him was Life, and the Life was the Light of men. And the Light shineth in the darkness, and the darkness apprehended it not.

There came a man sent from God, whose name was John. The same came as a witness, that he might bear witness of the Light, that all might believe through him. He was not the Light, but came to bear witness of the Light. That was the true Light which enlighteneth every man coming into this world. He was in the world, and the world was made through him, and the world knew him not. He came unto his own possessions, and they who were his own received him not. But as many as received him, to them gave he power to become the sons of God, even to them that believe in his name, who were born, not of blood, nor of the will of the flesh, nor of the will of man, but of God. And the Word was made flesh, and dwelt among us; (and we beheld his glory, the glory as of the Only-Begotten of the Father); full of grace and truth.

John beareth witness of him, and crieth out, saying; this is he of whom I said: he that cometh after me is preferred before me; for he was before me. And of his fulness have all we received, and grace for grace. For the law was given by Moses; grace and truth came by Jesus Christ. No man hath seen God at any time; the Only-Begotten Son who is in the bosom of the Father, he hath declared him.

And this is the testimony of John, when the Jews sent priests and Levites from

Jerusalem, to ask him, who art thou? And he confessed and denied not, and he confessed: I am not the Christ. And they asked him, what then? Art thou Elijah? And he said: I am not. Art thou the Prophet? And he answered: no. They said therefore unto him: who art thou? that we may give an answer to them that have sent us. What sayest thou of thyself? He said: I am the voice of one crying in the wilderness: make straight the way of the Lord; as said the prophet Isaiah. And they that were sent were of the Pharisees. And they asked him, and said unto him: why then dost thou baptize, if thou be not the Christ, nor Elijah, nor the Prophet? John answered them, saying: I baptize in water; but there hath stood in the midst of you, one whom you know not. The same is he, who coming after me, is preferred before me, the latchet of whose shoe I am not worthy to unloose.

These things were done in Bethany, beyond the Jordan, where John was baptizing.

On the morrow, John seeth Jesus coming

unto him, and saith: behold the Lamb of God; behold, this is he who taketh away the sin of the world. This is he of whom I said: after me cometh a man who is preferred before me; for he was before me. And I knew him not; but that he should be made manifest in Israel, therefore am I come, baptizing in water. And John bare witness, saying: I saw the Spirit coming down from heaven like a dove, and it abode upon him. And I knew him not, but he that sent me to baptize in water, the same said unto me: upon whom thou shalt see the Spirit coming down and abiding on him, the same is he who baptizeth in the Holy Spirit. And I saw and bare witness, that this is the Son of God.

The next day after, John was again standing with two of his disciples. And looking upon Jesus as he walked, he saith: behold, the Lamb of God! And the two disciples heard him speak, and they followed Jesus. Then Jesus turning and seeing them following him, saith unto them: what seek ye? They said unto him: Rabbi,

Peace be to this house.—*St. Luke x. 5.*

(which is to say, being interpreted, Master) where dwellest thou? He saith unto them: come and see. They came, and saw where he dwelt, and abode with him that day: now it was about the tenth hour. One of the two who had heard from John and had followed him was Andrew, Simon Peter's brother. He findeth first his own brother Simon, and saith unto him: we have found the Messiah (which is, being interpreted, the Christ). And he brought him to Jesus. Jesus, looking upon him, said: thou art Simon, the Son of Jona; thou shalt be called Cephas, which being interpreted, is Peter. The day following, Jesus would go forth into Galilee, and findeth Philip, and saith unto him: follow me! Now, Philip was of Bethsaida, the city of Andrew and Peter. Philip findeth Nathanael, and saith unto him: we have found him of whom Moses wrote in the Law, and the prophets; Jesus the son of Joseph of Nazareth. And Nathanael said unto him: can there any good thing come out of Nazareth? Philip saith unto him: come and see! Jesus saw

Nathanael coming unto him, and saith of him: behold, an Israelite indeed, in whom is no guile! Nathanael saith unto him: whence knowest thou me? Jesus answered and said unto him: before that Philip called thee, when thou wast underneath the fig-tree, I saw thee. Nathanael answered and said unto him: Rabbi, thou art the Son of God, thou art the King of Israel! Jesus answered and said unto him: because I said unto thee, I saw thee underneath the fig-tree, believest thou? Thou shalt see greater than these things. And he saith unto him: verily, verily, I say unto you: ye shall see the heaven opened, and the angels of God ascending and descending upon the Son of Man.

And the third day there was a wedding in Cana of Galilee, and the Mother of Jesus was there. And Jesus also, with his disciples, was bidden to the wedding. And the wine failing, the mother of Jesus saith to him: they have no wine. And Jesus saith to her: woman, what hast thou to do with me? my hour is not yet come. His mother saith to the waiters: whatsoever he saith unto you, do it. Now there were set there six water-pots of stone, after the manner of the purifying of the Jews, containing two or three firkins apiece. Jesus saith to them: fill the water-pots with water. And they filled them up to the brim. And Jesus saith to them: draw out now and bear to the governor of the feast. And they bare it. And when the governor of the feast had tasted the water that was made wine, and knew not whence it was; (but the waiters who had drawn the water knew,) the governor of the feast calleth the bridegroom, and saith to him: every man, at the beginning, doth set forth good wine, and when men have drank freely, then that which is worse; but thou hast kept the good wine until now.

This beginning of his miracles did Jesus in Cana of Galilee, and manifested his glory; and his disciples believed in him. After this, he, and his mother, and his brethren, and his disciples, went down to

Capernaum; and they abode there, not many days.

Now, the Passover of the Jews was at hand, and Jesus went up to Jerusalem. And he found in the temple them that sold oxen and sheep and doves, and the changers of money sitting. And when he had made a sort of scourge of small cords, he drave them all out from the temple, and the sheep also, and the oxen, and he poured out the coin of the money-changers, and overturned their tables; and he said to them that sold doves: take these things hence, and make not my Father's house a house of traffic. And his disciples remembered that it is written: the zeal of thine house hath eaten me up. The Jews, therefore, answered and said unto him: what sign showest thou unto us, seeing that thou doest these things? Jesus answered and said unto them: destroy this temple, and in three days I will raise it up. Then said the Jews: forty and six years was this temple in building, and wilt thou raise it up in three days? But he spake of the temple of his body. When therefore he had risen from the dead, his disciples remembered that he had said this, and they believed in the Scripture, and in the word which Jesus had spoken.

Now, while he was in Jerusalem, at the Passover, on the feast-day, many believed in his name, seeing his signs which he wrought. But Jesus did not trust himself to them, for he knew them all, and for that he needed not that any others should give testimony of any man; for he himself knew what was in man.

Now there was a man of the Pharisees named Nicodemus, a prince of the Jews. The same came to Jesus by night, and said unto him: Rabbi, we know that thou art come a teacher from God; for no one can do these signs which thou doest, unless God be with him. Jesus answered and said unto him: verily, verily, I say unto thee, except a man be born again, he cannot see the kingdom of God. Nicodemus saith unto him: how can a man be born when he is old? Can he enter a second time into his mother's womb, and be born again? Jesus answered: verily, verily, I say unto thee: except a man be born again of water and the Holy Spirit, he cannot enter into the kingdom of God. That which is born of the flesh is flesh, and that which is born of the Spirit is spirit. Marvel not that I said unto thee: ye must be born anew. The Spirit breatheth where he willeth, and thou hearest his voice, but thou knowest not whence he cometh nor whither he goeth; so is every one who is born of the Spirit. Nicodemus answered and said unto him: how can these things be done? Jesus answered and said unto him: thou art the teacher in Israel, and knowest thou not these things? Verily, verily, I say unto thee; that we speak what we know, and testify what we have seen, and ye receive not our testimony. If I have spoken unto you earthly things, and ye believe not, how will ye believe, if I speak unto you heavenly things? And no man hath ascended into heaven, but he that descended from

He took her by the hand and the maid arose.—*St. Matthew ix. 25.*

heaven, the Son of Man, who is in heaven. And as Moses lifted up the serpent in the desert, so must the Son of Man be lifted up, that whosoever believeth in him may not perish, but may have life everlasting. For God so loved the world, that he gave his Only-Begotten Son, that whosoever believeth in him may not perish, but may have life everlasting. For God sent not his Son into the world to judge the world; but that the world may be saved through him. He that believeth in him is not judged, but he that doth not believe is already judged; because he believeth not in the name of the Only-Begotten Son of God. And this is the judgment; that the Light hath come into the world, and men have loved the darkness rather than the Light, because their deeds were evil. For every one that doeth evil hateth the Light, neither cometh to the Light, lest his deeds should be reproved. But he that doeth truth cometh to the Light, that his deeds may be made manifest, that they are wrought in God.

After these things Jesus and his disciples

came into the land of Judea; and there he tarried with them and baptized. And John also was baptizing in Ennon near to Salim; because there was much water there; and they came and were baptized. For John had not yet been cast into prison. There arose therefore a questioning between some disciples of John and the Jews about purifying. And they came to John and said unto him: Rabbi, he who was with thee beyond the Jordan, to whom thou didst bear witness, behold the same baptizeth, and all men come unto him. John answered and said: a man can receive nothing except it be given unto him from heaven. Ye yourselves bear me witness, that I said: I am not the Christ, but, that I am sent before him. He that hath the bride is the bridegroom; but the friend of the bridegroom who standeth by, and heareth him, rejoiceth greatly at the voice of the bridegroom. This my joy, therefore, is fulfilled. He must increase, but I must decrease. He that cometh from above is over all. He that is of the earth is of the earth, and of the earth he speaketh. He that cometh from heaven is over all. What he hath seen and heard, of that he beareth witness, and no man receiveth his witness. He that hath received his witness, hath set his seal to attest that God is true. For he whom God hath sent speaketh the words of God, for God giveth him not the Spirit by measure. The Father loveth the Son, and hath given all things into his hand. Whosoever believeth in the Son hath life everlasting, but whosoever believeth not the Son shall not see life, but the wrath of God abideth on him.

When therefore Jesus knew how the Pharisees had heard that Jesus was making and baptizing more disciples than John, (though Jesus himself baptized not, but his disciples,) he left Judea and departed again into Galilee. And he must needs go through Samaria. Then cometh he to a city of Samaria called Sychar, near to the parcel of ground that Jacob gave to his son Joseph. Now Jacob's fountain was there. Jesus therefore, being wearied with his journey, sat accordingly beside the fountain. It was about the sixth hour. There cometh a woman of Samaria to draw water. Jesus saith unto her: give me to drink. (For his disciples had gone away into the city to buy food.) Then saith that Samaritan woman unto him: how is it that thou, being a Jew, askest drink of me, who am a woman of Samaria? (for Jews have no dealings with Samaritans.) Jesus answered and said unto her: if thou knewest the gift of God, and who it is that saith to thee, give me to drink; thou wouldst perhaps have asked of him, and he would have given thee living water. The woman saith to him: sir, thou hast nothing to draw with, and the well is deep; whence, therefore, hast thou that living water? Art thou greater than our father Jacob, that gave us the well, and drank thereof, himself, and his children, and his cattle? Jesus answered and said unto her: whosoever drinketh of this water, shall thirst again; but whosoever drinketh of the water that I will give him,

She had a sister called Mary, who sitting also at the Lord's feet, heard his word.—*St. Luke x. 39.*

shall never thirst; but the water that I will give him shall be in him a fountain of water springing up into everlasting life. The woman saith unto him: sir, give me this water, that I thirst not, neither come hither to draw. Jesus saith unto her: go call thy husband, and come hither. The woman answered and said: I have no husband. Jesus saith unto her: thou hast well said, I have no husband; for thou hast had five husbands, and he whom thou now hast is not thy husband; in that saidst thou truly. The woman saith unto him: sir, I perceive that thou art a prophet. Our fathers worshipped in this mountain, and ye say, that in Jerusalem is the place where men ought to worship. Jesus saith unto her: woman, believe me the hour cometh, when ye shall neither in this mountain, nor at Jerusalem, worship the Father. Ye worship, ye know not what; we know what we worship, for salvation is of the Jews. But the hour cometh, and now is, when the true worshippers shall worship the Father in spirit and in truth. For the Father seeketh such to worship him. God is a Spirit, and they that worship him must worship in spirit and in truth. The woman saith unto him: I know that Messiah cometh, (who is called Christ;) when he is come he will tell us all things. Jesus saith unto her: I that speak unto thee am he. And upon this came his disciples, and marvelled that he was speaking with a woman; yet no man said, what seekest thou? or why speakest thou with her? The woman then left her water-pot, and went her way into the city, and saith to the men: come see a man who told me all things whatsoever that I have done. Is this the Christ? Then they went out of the city, and while they were on the way to him, his disciples in the meantime prayed him, saying: Master, eat. But he saith unto them: I have food to eat that ye know not of. Therefore said the disciples one to another: hath any man brought him aught to eat? Jesus saith unto them: my food is to do the will of him that sent me, that I may finish his work. Say not ye, there are yet four months, and then cometh harvest? Behold, I say unto you: lift up your eyes, and look on the fields: for they are white already unto harvest. And he that reapeth receiveth wages, and gathereth fruit unto life eternal, that both he that soweth, and he that reapeth, may rejoice together. And herein is that saying true; one soweth, and another reapeth. I have sent you to reap that whereon ye bestowed no labor; other men labored, and ye are entered into their labors. And many of the Samaritans of that city believed in him for the saying of the woman who testified, he told me all things whatsoever I have done. So when the Samaritans were come unto him, they besought him that he would remain with them; and he abode there two days. And many more believed because of his own word; and they said unto the woman: now we believe, not because of thy saying; for we have heard him ourselves, and we know that this is, indeed, the Saviour of the world.

Now, after two days, he departed thence, and went into Galilee. For Jesus himself bore witness, that a prophet hath no honor in his own country. When he was come, then, into Galilee, the Galileans received him, having seen all the things that he did at Jerusalem, at the feast; for they also went unto the feast.

He came, therefore, again unto Cana of Galilee, where he made the water wine. And there was a certain king's officer, whose son was sick at Capernaum. When he heard that Jesus was come out of Judea into Galilee, he went unto him and besought him that he would come down and heal his son, for he was at the point of death. Then said Jesus unto him, except ye see signs and wonders, ye do not believe. The king's officer saith unto him: sir, come down, before that my son die. Jesus saith unto him: go thy way, thy son liveth. The man believed the word that Jesus had spoken unto him, and he went his way. And as he was now going down, his servants met him, and told him, saying: thy son liveth. Then inquired he of them the hour when he began to amend. And they

But she hath washed my feet with tears and wiped them with hairs of her head.—*St. Luke vii. 44.*

said to him, yesterday at the seventh hour the fever left him. So the father knew that it was the same hour in which Jesus said to him: thy son liveth; and he himself believed, and his whole house. This is again the second miracle Jesus wrought, when he was come out of Judea into Galilee.

After these things was a festival day of the Jews, and Jesus went up to Jerusalem. Now there is at Jerusalem a pool, Probatica, which in Hebrew is named Bethsaida, having five porches. In these lay a great multitude of sick, of blind, of lame, of withered, waiting for the stirring of the water. For an angel of the Lord went down at certain times into the pool, and the water was stirred. And whosoever first went down into the pool after the stirring of the water, was made whole of whatever infirmity he suffered. And there was a certain man there who had been eight and thirty years under his infirmity. When Jesus saw him lying there, and knew that he had been there for a long time, he saith unto him: wilt thou be made whole? The infirm man answered him: sir, I have no man, when the water is troubled, to put me into the pool; but while I am coming, another steppeth down before me. Jesus saith unto him: arise, take up thy bed, and walk. And immediately the man was made whole, and took up his bed, and walked. And on the same day was the sabbath. The Jews therefore said unto him that was cured: it is the sabbath day; it is not lawful for thee to carry thy bed. He answered them: he that made me whole, the same said unto me, take up thy bed, and walk. Then asked they him: who is that man who said to thee, take up thy bed, and walk? But he who was healed knew not who it was; for Jesus had gone aside from the crowd gathered in the place. Afterwards, Jesus findeth him in the temple, and he saith unto him: now thou art made whole; sin not, henceforth, lest some worse thing befall thee. The man departed, and told to the Jews that it was Jesus who made him whole.

Therefore the Jews persecuted Jesus, because he did these things on the sabbath. But Jesus answered them: my Father worketh until now, and I work. For this reason, therefore, the Jews sought the more to kill him, because he not only brake the sabbath, but also called God his own Father; making himself equal to God. Jesus, therefore, answered and said to them: verily, verily, I say unto you. the Son cannot do anything of himself, but what he seeth the Father doing; for what things soever he doeth, these the Son also in like manner doeth. For the Father loveth the Son, and showeth unto him all things which himself doeth; and greater works than these will he show him, that ye may marvel. For as the Father raiseth the dead and quickeneth them, even so, the Son also quickeneth whom he will. For neither doth the Father judge any man, but he hath given all judgment unto the Son; that all may honor the Son, even as they honor the Father. He that honoreth not the Son, honoreth not the Father who hath sent him. Verily,

verily, I say unto you: that he who heareth my word, and believeth him who sent me, hath life everlasting, and cometh not into judgment, but hath passed from death to life. Verily, verily, I say unto you: that the hour cometh, and now is, when the dead shall hear the voice of the Son of God: and they who hear, shall live. For, as the Father hath life in himself, so also he hath given to the Son to have life in himself; and he hath given him power to execute judgment, because he is the Son of Man. Marvel not at this; for the hour is coming in which all who are in the graves will hear the voice of the Son of God, and will come forth; they who have done good things to the resurrection of life, and they who have done evil things to the resurrection of judgment. I cannot do anything of myself. As I hear, I judge; and my judgment is just, because I seek not mine own will, but the will of him who sent me. If I bear witness of myself, my witness is not true. There is another who beareth witness of me, and I know that the witness which

And he that was dead sat up and began to speak. And he delivered him to his mother.—*St. Luke vii. 15.*

he witnesseth of me is true. Ye sent unto John, and he bare witness unto the truth. I receive not, indeed, testimony from man, but I say these things that ye may be saved. He was the lamp that burneth and shineth. And ye were willing to rejoice for an hour in his light. But I have a greater than John's witness. For the works which the Father hath given me to finish, those very works which I do bear witness of me, that the Father hath sent me. And the Father himself who sent me hath borne witness of me. Ye have neither heard his voice at any time, nor have ye seen his form, and his word ye have not abiding in you; for whom he hath sent, him ye believe not. Ye search the Scriptures, because in them ye think to have eternal life, and the same are they which bear witness of me; and ye will not come to me, that ye may have life. I receive not glory from men; but I have known you, that ye have not the love of God in you. I have come in the name of my Father, and ye receive me not; if another shall come in his own name, him ye will receive. How can ye believe, who receive honor one from another, and seek not the glory which is from God only? Do not think that I will accuse you to the Father. There is one who accuseth you, Moses, in whom ye trust. For, had ye believed Moses, ye would doubtless also have believed me; for he wrote of me. But, if ye believe not his writings, how shall ye believe my words.

After these things, Jesus went over the sea of Galilee, which is the sea of Tiberias. And a great multitude followed him, because they saw the miracles which he wrought on them that were diseased. And Jesus went up into a mountain, and there he sat with his disciples. Now the Passover, (the festival day of the Jews,) was nigh. When, therefore, Jesus had lifted up his eyes and had seen that a very great multitude came unto him, he said to Philip: whence shall we buy loaves of bread, that these may eat? And this he said to prove him, for he himself knew what he would do. Philip answered him: two hundred denarii worth of loaves would not suffice for them, to give each one a morsel. One of his disciples, Andrew, Simon Peter's brother, said: there is a little lad here, who hath five barley loaves, and two fishes, but what are these among so many? Then Jesus said: make the men sit down. Now there was much grass in the place. So, the men sat down, and they were in number about five thousand. Jesus then took the loaves, and when he had given thanks he distributed them to the men who were seated around, and of the fishes in like manner, giving all as much as they wished for. And when they had taken their fill, he said to his disciples: gather up the fragments which are left, that they may not be wasted. They gathered up, therefore, the fragments of the five barley loaves left over with those who had eaten, and they filled with them twelve baskets.

Those men, therefore, when they had seen what a miracle Jesus had wrought, said: this is, of a truth, the prophet that is to come into the world. Jesus, therefore, perceiving that they were about to come and take him by force to make him king, withdrew again into the mountain, himself alone. And when evening was come, his disciples went down to the sea. And having entered into a vessel, they were going across the sea to Capernaum; and it was now dark, and Jesus was not come to them. And the sea was rising, by reason of a high wind that blew. When, therefore, they had rowed about five and twenty or thirty furlongs, they behold Jesus walking on the sea, and drawing nigh unto the vessel, and they were afraid. But he saith to them: it is I; be not afraid. They would therefore have him come into the vessel; and, presently, the vessel was at the land whither they were going.

On the morrow, the multitude which was staying on the other side of the sea, saw that there was no other vessel there, save the one, and that Jesus had not entered into the vessel with his disciples, but his disciples had departed alone. Howbeit,

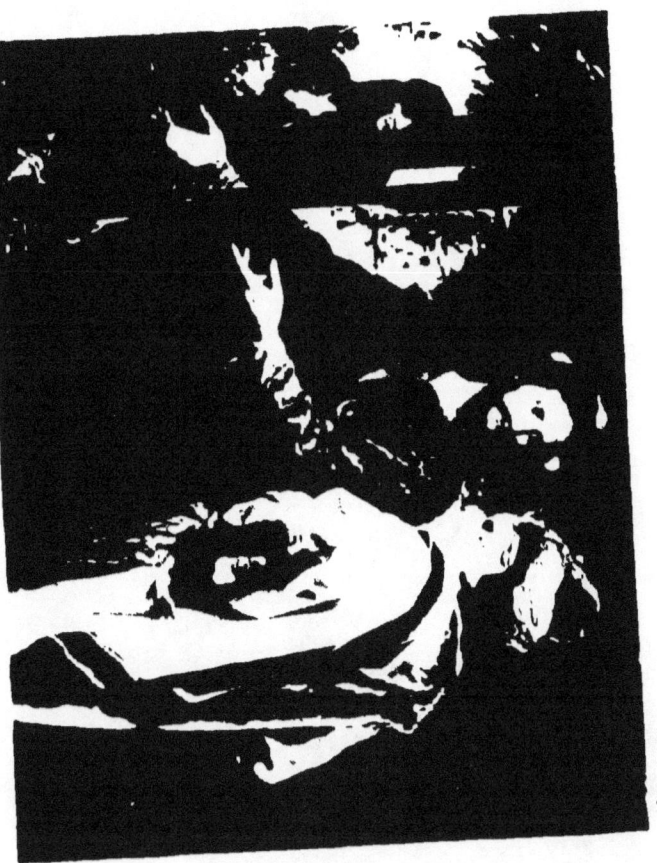

If thou wilt be perfect, go and sell what thou hast, and give to the poor.
—*St. Matthew* xix. 21.

other boats came in from Tiberias, nigh unto the place where they had eaten the bread after the Lord had given thanks. When, therefore, the multitude had seen that Jesus was not there, nor his disciples, they betook themselves to the boats and came to Capernaum seeking for Jesus. And when they had found him on the other side of the sea, they said unto him: Rabbi, when camest thou hither? Jesus answered them and said: verily, verily, I say unto you; ye seek me not because ye saw the miracles, but because ye ate of the loaves and were filled. Labor not for the food which perisheth, but for that which endureth unto life everlasting, which the Son of Man will give unto you; for him the Father, even God, hath sealed. They said therefore unto him: what shall we do, that we may work the works of God? Jesus answered and said unto them: this is the work of God, that ye believe in him whom he hath sent. They said therefore unto him: what doest thou for a sign, that we may see and believe thee? What dost thou work? Our fathers ate manna in the desert, as it is written: he gave them bread from heaven to eat. Jesus then said to them: verily, verily, I say unto you; Moses did not give you the bread from heaven, but my Father giveth you the true bread from heaven. For that is the bread of God, which cometh down from heaven and giveth life to the world. Then said they unto him: Lord, evermore give us this bread. And Jesus said unto them: I am the bread of life; he that cometh to me shall not hunger, and he that believeth in me shall never thirst. But, as I said to you; ye have both seen me, and yet do not believe. All that the Father giveth me shall come unto me, and him that cometh to me I will not cast out; because I am come down from heaven, not that I may do mine own will, but the will of him who sent me. Now, this is the will of him who sent me, even the Father; that of all which he hath given me I lose nothing, but that I raise it up again on the last day. And this is the will of my Father who sent me; that every one who seeth the Son and believeth in him may have life eternal, and I will raise him up on the last day. The Jews therefore murmured at him, because he had said: I am the living bread which came down from heaven. And they said: is not this Jesus, the son of Joseph, whose father and mother we know? how is it then that he saith, I am come down from heaven? Jesus therefore answered and said unto them: murmur not among yourselves. No one can come unto me, unless the Father who hath sent me draw him, and I will raise him up again on the last day. It is written in the prophets: and they shall all be taught of God. Every man, therefore, that hath heard and learned of the Father cometh unto me. Not that any man hath seen the Father, save he who is of God; he hath seen the Father. Verily, verily, I say unto you: he that believeth in me hath everlasting life. I am the bread of life. Your fathers ate manna in the desert, and they died. This is the bread which cometh down from heaven, that if a man eat thereof, he will not die. I am the living bread which came down from heaven. If any man eat of this bread he shall live for ever, and the bread which I will give is my flesh, for the life of the world. The Jews therefore strove among themselves, saying: how can this man give us his flesh to eat? Whereupon Jesus said to them: verily, verily, I say unto you, unless ye eat the flesh of the Son of Man, and drink his blood, ye shall not have life in yourselves. Whoso eateth my flesh and drinketh my blood, hath everlasting life, and I will raise him up on the last day. For my flesh is truly food, and my blood is truly drink. Whoso eateth my flesh and drinketh my blood, abideth in me, and I in him. As the living Father hath sent me, and I live because of the Father: so also whoso eateth me, even he shall live because of me. This is the bread which came down from heaven; not as your fathers ate manna and died. Whoso eateth this bread shall live for ever.

These things said he, as he was teaching in the synagogue in Capernaum.

"But a certain Samaritan, as he journeyed, came where he was, and had compassion on him."—*St. Luke* x. 33.

Whereupon, many of his disciples who were listening to him, said: this is a hard saying, and who can give ear to it? But Jesus, knowing in himself that His disciples murmured about this, said to them: doth this cause you to stumble? What, then, if ye should behold the Son of Man ascending up where he was before? It is the spirit that maketh alive, the flesh profiteth nothing; the words that I have spoken to you are spirit and life. But there are some of you who do not believe. For Jesus knew from the beginning who they were that believed not, and who would betray him. And he said: therefore I said to you: that no man can come to me, except it were given to him from my Father. Upon this, many of his disciples went back, and walked no more with him. Then Jesus said to the twelve: would ye also go away? Whereupon Simon Peter answered him: Lord, to whom shall we go? thou hast the words of eternal life. And we have believed, and we know that thou art the Christ, the Son of God. Jesus answered to them; have I not chosen you twelve, and one of you is a devil? Now he meant Judas Iscariot the son of Simon, for it was this man who was to betray him, being one of the twelve.

And after these things Jesus walked in Galilee, for he would not walk in Judea, because the Jews sought to kill him. Now a feast of the Jews, the Feast of Tabernacles, was at hand. And his brethren said to him: depart hence and go into Judea, that thy disciples also may see thy works which thou doest. For no man doeth anything in secret, and seeketh to be himself known openly. If thou doest these things, manifest thyself to the world. For neither did his brethren believe in him. Jesus therefore saith unto them: my time hath not yet come, but your time is always at hand. The world cannot hate you, but me it hateth, because I bear witness of it, that its deeds are evil. Go ye up to this festival day; but I go not up to this festival day, because my time is not yet fulfilled. When he had said these things, he remained in Galilee. But when his brethren had gone up, then he went up himself, to the feast, not openly, but as it were in secret. The Jews therefore sought for him at the feast, and said: where is he? And there was much whispered talk among the multitude because of him; for some said, he is a good man, while others said: nay, but he seduceth the people. Howbeit, no man spake openly of him, for fear of the Jews. Now, about the middle of the feast Jesus went up into the temple and taught. And the Jews marvelled; saying: how knoweth this man letters, having never learned? Jesus answered them and said: my doctrine is not mine, but his that sent me. If any man will do his will, he will know of the doctrine whether it be of God, or whether I speak of myself. He that speaketh of himself, seeketh his own glory; but he who seeketh the glory of him that sent him, the same is true, and there is no unrighteousness in him. Did not Moses give you the law, yet no one of you observeth the law?

Why do you seek to kill me? The multitude answered and said: thou hast a devil; who seeketh to kill thee? Jesus answered and said unto them: one work have I done, and ye all marvel; nevertheless, Moses gave unto you circumcision, (not that it is of Moses, but of the fathers,) and ye on the sabbath day circumcise a man. If a man receive circumcision on the sabbath day, that the law of Moses may not be broken, are ye wroth with me because I have made a man every whit whole on the sabbath day? Judge not according to the appearance, but judge just judgment. Some therefore of Jerusalem said: is not this he whom they seek to put to death? yet he discourseth openly, and they say nothing to him. Have the rulers then come to know that he is truly the Christ? But we know this man, whence he is; whereas, when Christ cometh, no one knoweth whence he is. Thereupon, Jesus exclaimed aloud in the temple, teaching and saying: ye both know me, and whence I am, ye know; and I have not come of myself, but he is true

He began to cast them out that sold therein, and them that bought,
—*St. Luke xix. 45.*

who hath sent me, whom ye know not. I know him, because I am from him, and he hath sent me. Therefore, they sought to apprehend him, but no one laid hands on him, because his hour was not yet come. But many of the people believed in him, and said: when the Christ cometh, will he do more miracles than this man doeth? The Pharisees overheard the multitude whispering these things concerning him; and the rulers and Pharisees sent officers to apprehend him. Jesus accordingly said to them: yet a little while I am with you, and I go to him that sent me. Ye shall seek me and ye shall not find me, and where I am ye cannot come. Then said the Jews among themselves: whither will he go, that we shall not find him? Will he go into the dispersion of the gentiles, and teach the gentiles? What manner of saying is this which he hath said: ye shall seek me and shall not find me; and, where I go, there ye cannot come?

Now, on the last day, the great day of the feast, Jesus stood and cried, saying:

if any·man thirst, let him come unto me and drink. He that believeth in me, as the Scripture saith, from within him shall flow rivers of living water. But this spake he of the Spirit, which they that believe in him should receive; for the Spirit was not yet given, because Jesus was not yet glorified. Some of that multitude, when they had heard these sayings of his, said: this is, of a truth, the Prophet; others said: this is the Christ; but some said: what! doth the Christ come out of Galilee? Doth not the Scripture say: that the Christ cometh from the seed of David, and from the village of Bethlehem, where David was? So there arose a dissension among the people because of him. And some of them would have taken him; but no man did lay hands on him.

Then came the officers to the chief priests and Pharisees; and they said unto them: why have ye not brought him? The officers answered: never man spake like this man. The Pharisees answered them: are ye also led astray? Hath any one of the rulers or of the Pharisees believed in him? But this rabble that knoweth not the law are accursed. Nicodemus said to them: (the same who came to him by night, who was one of them,) doth our law, then, judge a man, unless it hath first heard from himself, and hath known what he doeth? They answered and said unto him: what then, art thou also a Galilean? Search the Scriptures, and see; for out of Galilee ariseth no prophet. And they departed, each one to his own house.

And Jesus went unto Mount Olivet; and early in the morning he came again into the temple, and all the people came unto him; and he sat down and taught them. And the Scribes and Pharisees brought unto him a woman taken in adultery; and they sat her in the midst, and said to him: Master, this woman was just now taken in adultery. Now, Moses in the law commanded us, that such should be stoned. But what sayest thou? This they said tempting him, that they might find whereof to accuse him. But Jesus, stooping down wrote with his finger on the ground. And when they continued questioning him, he raised himself up, and said to them: he that is without sin among you let him first cast a stone at her. And again stooping down, he wrote on the ground. But they, upon hearing his words, went out, one after another, beginning with the eldest; and Jesus remained alone, and the woman where she was in the midst. Then Jesus raising himself up, said to her: woman, where are they who accused thee? Hath no man condemned thee? She said: no man, Lord. And Jesus said: neither will I condemn thee; go, and henceforth sin no more.

Then spake Jesus again unto them, saying: I am the light of the world; he that followeth me walketh not in darkness, but shall have the light of life. The Pharisees therefore said unto him: thou bearest witness of thyself; thy witness is not true. Jesus answered and said unto them: and even if I do bear witness of myself, my testimony is true, because I know whence I came, and whither I go; but ye know not whence I came, or whither I go. Ye judge according to the flesh; I judge no man; and yet if I judge, my judgment is true, for I am not alone, but I and the Father who sent me. It is also written in your law that the testimony of two men is true. I am one that bear witness of myself, and the Father who sent me beareth witness of me. They said therefore unto him: where is thy Father? Jesus answered: ye neither know me nor my Father. If ye had known me, ye might have known my Father also. These words spake Jesus in the treasury, as he was teaching in the temple; and no man laid hands on him, for his hour was not yet come.

Then said Jesus again unto them: I go away, and ye shall seek me, and ye shall die in your sin. Whither I go, ye cannot come. Then said the Jews: will he kill himself? Because he said, whither I go ye cannot come. And he said unto them: ye are from beneath; I am from above; ye are of this world; I am not of this world. Therefore I said to you, that ye shall die in your sins; for if ye believe not that I Am, ye shall die in your sin. They said therefore unto him: who art thou? Jesus said to them: The Beginning who also speak to you.*

---

* This sentence is extremely obscure, on account of its elliptical construction, the principal noun, both in the Greek and Latin text, which translated into English is "the beginning," being in the accusative, and not, as in the version given above, in the nominative. King James's version and the revision of it, as well as most moderns, explain it as if Christ said "I am what I told you from the beginning." This is a gloss or a paraphrase and not a literal rendering, which cannot be given in English, so as to make an intelligible sense. A paraphrase is evidently necessary. St. Augustine has given one which is intelligibly expressed by assuming the noun "beginning' as a nominative.

The ancient Latin text which he quotes reads: *Principium quia* (instead of *qui*) *et loquor vobis;* which is, however, immaterial in respect to the sense of his paraphrase. "*Principium*" being an accusative, is supposed to be governed by a verb understood. "Since he perceived that they demanded, who art thou? as if saying to him, since we have heard you threaten us, if ye do not believe that I Am; what shall we believe you to be? He answered, 'the beginning : as if he said, believe me to be the beginning, and added, 'for I also speak to you'; that is, having humbled myself on your account, I have come to declare it."

If the Greek accusative is taken as governed by a verb understood, so as to make the meaning " believe me to be the Beginning, who am the first principle and cause of the creation, and also the Word made flesh, seen by you, and speaking to you, with an audible human voice"; then "*Principium qui et loquor vobis*," taking "*principium*" as a nominative, and " *The* Beginning who also speak to you," tersely and correctly express the genuine sense of the authentic text of the Evangelist. (See *Kenrick, in loc.*)

It is written again, Thou shalt not tempt the Lord thy God.—*St. Matthew iv. 7.*

I have many things to say and to judge of you, but he who sent me is true; and I speak to the world those things which I have heard of him. And they understood not that he called God his Father. Then said Jesus unto them: when ye have lifted up the Son of Man, then shall ye know that I AM, and that I do nothing of myself; but as my Father hath taught me, I speak these things. And he that sent me is with me, and hath not left me alone; for I do always the things that are pleasing to him.

As he thus discoursed, many believed in him. Then Jesus said to those Jews who believed him: if ye abide in my word, ye will be my disciples indeed, and ye will know the truth, and the truth will make you free. They answered him: we are the seed of Abraham, and were never in bondage to any man; how sayest thou then, ye shall be made free? Jesus answered them: verily, verily, I say unto you; whosoever committeth sin is the slave of sin. But the slave abideth not in the house for ever;

the Son, however, doth abide therein for ever.

If the Son, therefore, shall make you free, ye shall be free indeed. I know that ye are Abraham's children; but ye seek to kill me, because my word doth not take root in you. I speak what I have seen with my Father; and ye do the things ye have seen with your father. They answered and said unto him: Abraham is our father. Jesus saith unto them: if ye are Abraham's children, do the works of Abraham. But now, ye seek to kill me, a man who have spoken unto you the truth which I have heard from God; this did not Abraham. Ye do the deeds of your father. They said therefore to him: we are not born of fornication; we have one Father, God. Jesus therefore said to them: if God were your Father, ye would surely love me. For I proceeded forth and came from God; for I came not of myself, but he sent me. Why do ye not recognize my speech? Because ye cannot give ear to my doctrine. Ye are of your father, the devil, and the desires of your father ye wish to fulfil. He was a manslayer from the beginning, and he abode not in the truth, for truth is not in him. When he speaketh a lie, he speaketh of his own; for he is a liar and the father thereof. But if I speak the truth, ye do not believe me. Which of you shall convict me of sin? If I speak truth to you, why do ye not believe me? He that is of God heareth God's words; ye, therefore, hear them not, because ye are not of God. The Jews therefore answered and said unto him: say we not well that thou art a Samaritan and hast a demon? Jesus answered: I have not a demon; but I honor my Father, and ye have dishonored me. But I seek not mine own glory; there is one that seeketh it and giveth judgment. Verily, verily, I say unto you: if any man keep my word, he shall not see death for ever. The Jews therefore said: now we know that thou hast a demon. Abraham is dead, and the prophets. And thou sayest: if any man keep my word, he shall not taste death for ever. Art thou greater than our father Abraham, who is dead? And the prophets are dead. Whom makest thou thyself? Jesus answered: if I glorify myself, my glory is nothing; it is my Father that glorifieth me, of whom ye say that he is your God; and ye have not known him; but I have known him. And if I should say that I know him not, I shall be like yourselves, a liar; but I do know him, and I keep his word. Abraham your father eagerly desired that he might see my day; he saw it, and he rejoiced. The Jews therefore said to him: thou art not yet fifty years old, and hast thou seen Abraham? Jesus said to them: verily, verily, I say unto you: before Abraham was made, I Am. They took up stones, therefore, to cast at him; but Jesus hid himself and went out of the temple.

And Jesus passing by, saw a man who was blind from his birth. And his disciples questioned him, saying: Rabbi, who hath sinned, this man or his parents, that he should be born blind? Jesus answered:

neither hath this man sinned, nor his parents, but that the works of God should be made manifest in him. I must work the works of him that sent me while it is day; the night cometh, wherein no man can work. As long as I am in the world, I am the light of the world.

When he had said these things, he spat on the ground, and made clay of the spittle, and rubbed the clay upon his eyes, and said to him: go, wash in the pool of Siloe, (which is interpreted Sent.) He went away, therefore, and washed, and came back seeing. The neighbors therefore, and they that had seen him before, for he was a beggar, said: is not this he who used to sit and beg? Some said: it is he. Others again said: not at all, but it is some one who is like him. But he said: I am the man. They said therefore to him: how have thine eyes been opened? He answered: that man who is called Jesus made clay and anointed mine eyes, and said to me, go wash in the pool of Siloe. And I went, and I washed, and I see. And they said to him: where is he? He saith: I know not. They bring him who had been blind to the Pharisees. Now, it was the sabbath when Jesus made clay and opened his eyes. So then, the Pharisees questioned him once more, how he had got his eyesight. And he said to them: he put clay upon mine eyes, and I washed, and I see. Whereupon some of the Pharisees said: this man is not from God, who keepeth not the sabbath; but others said: how can a man who is a sinner work these miracles? And there was division among them. They say therefore again to the blind man: what dost thou say of him who opened thine eyes? And he said: he is a prophet. The Jews, nevertheless, did not believe that he had been blind and had been made to see, until they called the parents of him who had received his eyesight, and questioned them, saying: is this your son, who ye say was born blind? How then is he now seeing? His parents answered them, and said: we know that this is our son, and that he was born blind; but how it is that he is

Is it not written, My house shall be called the house of prayer to all nations? But you have made it a den of thieves.—*St. Mark* xi. 17.

now seeing, we know not; or who hath opened his eyes, we do not know: ask him, for he is of age, and let him speak for himself. These things said his parents, because they feared the Jews; for already the Jews had agreed among themselves, that if any one confessed him to be the Christ, he should be put out of the synagogue. Therefore did his parents say: he is of age, ask him. So they called again the man who had been blind, and said unto him: give glory to God; we know that this man is a sinner. He said then unto them: whether he be a sinner, I know not; one thing I do know, that whereas I had been blind, I now can see. They said therefore unto him: what did he do to thee? how did he open thine eyes? He answered them: I have already told you, and ye have heard me; why do ye wish to hear it again? Is it that ye also wish to become his disciples? Thereupon they reviled him, and they said: be thou his disciple; but we are disciples of Moses. We know that God spake to Moses; but as for this man, we know not whence he is. The man answered and said unto them: why, herein is a wonderful thing; that ye do not know whence he is, whereas he hath opened mine eyes. We know, nevertheless, that God heareth not sinners; but that if any man be a worshipper of God and do his will, him he heareth. Since the world began, it hath not been heard of, that any one hath opened the eyes of one born blind. Unless this man were from God, he could not do anything. They answered and said unto him: thou wast wholly born in sins, and dost thou teach us? And they cast him out.

Jesus heard that they had cast him out; and when he had found him, he said unto him: dost thou believe in the Son of God?

He answered and said: who is he, Lord, that I may believe in him? And Jesus said unto him; thou hast both seen him, and he who talketh with thee is he. Then he saith: Lord, I believe. And falling down, he adored him. And Jesus said: for judgment I have come into this world, that they who see not, may see, and they who see may become blind. And some of the Pharisees who were with him heard this, and they said unto him: how then, are we also blind? Jesus said unto them: if ye were blind, ye would not have sin; but now that ye say: we see, your sin remaineth.

Verily, verily, I say unto you: he who entereth not by the door into the sheepfold, but climbeth up some other way, the same is a thief and a robber. But he who entereth by the door is the shepherd of the sheep. To him the gate-keeper openeth, and the sheep hear his voice, and he calleth his own sheep by name, and leadeth them forth. And when he leadeth forth his own sheep, he goeth before them, and the sheep follow him, because they know his voice. But a stranger they follow not, but flee from him, because they know not the voice of strangers. This similitude Jesus spake to them. But they understood not what he spake to them. Therefore Jesus said unto them again: verily, verily, I say unto you: that I am the door of the sheep. All, as many as have come before me are thieves and robbers, and the sheep heard them not. I am the door; if any man enter in by me, he shall be saved, and he shall go in, and go out, and find pastures. The thief cometh not, but to steal, and to kill, and to destroy. I am come that they may have life, and may have it more abundantly. I am the good shepherd. The good shepherd giveth his life for his sheep. But the hireling and he who is not the shepherd, whose own the sheep are not, seeth the wolf coming, and leaveth the sheep and fleeth; and the wolf seizeth and scattereth the sheep. But the hireling fleeth because he is a hireling and careth not for the sheep. I am the good shepherd, and I know mine, and mine know me; even as the Father knoweth me, and I know the Father; and I lay down my life for my sheep. And other sheep I have which are not of this fold; and them also I must bring, and they shall hear my voice, and there shall become one fold, and one shepherd. Therefore my Father loveth me, because I lay down my life, that I may take it up again. No man taketh it from me, but I lay it down of myself; and I have the power of laying it down, and the power of taking it up again. This commandment I have received of my Father.

Dissension arose again among the Jews, on account of these words. And many of them said: he hath a demon, and is mad; why hearken ye to him? Others said: these are not the sayings of one who hath a demon: can, indeed, a demon open the eyes of the blind?

Now the feast of the Dedication was kept in Jerusalem; and it was winter; and Jesus was walking in the temple, in Solomon's porch. The Jews accordingly surrounded him, and they said to him: how long dost thou hold our minds in suspense? If thou art the Christ, tell us plainly. Jesus answered them: I speak to you, and ye do not believe; the works which I do in the name of my Father, they bear witness of me. But ye believe not, because ye are not of my sheep, as I said unto you. My sheep hear my voice, and I know them, and they follow me, and I will give unto them eternal life: and they shall never perish, neither shall any one snatch them out of my hand. That which my Father hath given me is greater than all, and no one can snatch aught out of the hand of my Father. I and the Father are one.*

Then the Jews took up stones to stone him. Jesus answered them: many good works have I showed you from my Father; for which of those works do ye stone me? The Jews answered him: for a good work we stone thee not, but for blasphemy; and because that thou, whereas thou art a man, makest thyself God. Jesus answered them: is it not written in your law: I said: ye are gods? If he called those gods, unto whom the word of God came, (and the Scripture cannot be broken,) say ye of him whom the Father hath sanctified and sent into the world: thou blasphemest; because

---

* The adjective "one" is neuter in Greek and Latin. Literally, "one thing"—*i.e.*, "one essence and nature"; which explains why the Jews, when he said this, wished to stone him.

I said: I am the Son of God? If I do not the works of my Father, refuse to believe me. But if I do them, and if ye do not choose to believe me, believe the works; so that ye may know and believe, that the Father is in me, and I am in the Father. Therefore, they sought to lay hold on him, and he went forth out of their hands.

And he went away again beyond the Jordan to that place where John at first was baptizing, and he abode there. And many came unto him, and they said: John indeed wrought no miracle. But all things whatsoever John said of this man were true. And many believed in him.

Now there was a certain man named Lazarus, who was sick, of Bethany, the village of Mary and her sister Martha. (It was that Mary who anointed the Lord with ointment and wiped his feet with her hair, whose brother Lazarus was sick.) His sisters, therefore, sent unto him, saying: Lord, behold he whom thou lovest is sick. But Jesus, when he heard that, said to them;

this sickness is not unto death, but for the glory of God, that the Son of God may be glorified thereby. Now Jesus loved Martha, and her sister Mary, and Lazarus. When, therefore, he had heard that he was sick, he abode still in the same place for two days. And after this, he said to his disciples: let us go again into Judea. The disciples say unto him: Rabbi, the Jews were but now seeking to stone thee, and goest thou thither again? Jesus answered: are there not twelve hours in the day? If any one walketh in the daytime, he stumbleth not, because he seeth the light of this world; but if he walketh by night, he stumbleth, because he hath no light. These things saith he, and afterwards he said unto them: our friend Lazarus is asleep, but I am going, that I may arouse him from slumber. Therefore his disciples said: Lord, if he be sleeping, he will be doing well. Jesus, however, had spoken of his death; whereas they thought that he was speaking of the repose of sleep. Then Jesus, accordingly, said to them plainly:

Lazarus is dead. And I am glad for your sakes that I was not there, that ye may believe; but let us go to him. Thomas (the same who is called The Twin) said therefore to his fellow disciples: let us also go, that we may die with him.

Jesus therefore came, and found him already lying in the tomb for four days. (Now Bethany was near Jerusalem, at the distance of about fifteen furlongs.) And many of the Jews had come to visit Martha and Mary, and to console them concerning their brother. Martha, therefore, when she heard that Jesus was coming, went out in haste to meet him, while Mary remained seated in the house. Then said Martha to Jesus: Lord, if thou hadst been here, my brother would not have died; but I know that even now, whatever thou shalt ask of God, God will give it to thee. Jesus saith to her: thy brother shall rise again. Martha saith to him: I know that he will rise again in the resurrection, on the last day. Jesus said to her: I am the resurrection and the life; whoso believeth in me, although he were dead, shall live; and every one who liveth and believeth in me, shall not die for ever. Believest thou this? She saith to him: Yea, Lord, I have believed that thou art the Christ, the Son of the Living God, who hast come into this world. And when she had said this, she went away, and called her sister Mary, telling her secretly: the Master is come, and calleth for thee. When she heard this, she riseth up quickly and cometh forth to him; for Jesus had not yet come into the village; but he was still in the same place where Martha had met him. The Jews, therefore, who had been with her, and consoling her in the house, when they saw Mary, that she rose up hastily and went out, followed her, saying: she goeth unto the sepulchre to weep there. When Mary, therefore, was come where Jesus was, and saw him, she fell down at his feet, and saith to him: Lord, if thou hadst been here, my brother had not died. When Jesus therefore saw her weeping, and the Jews who had come with her weeping, he groaned in spirit and troubled himself. And he said: where have ye laid him? They say to him: Lord, come and see. And Jesus wept. Therefore the Jews said: behold how he loved him. And some of them said: could not he, who opened the eyes of one born blind, have caused that this man should not have died? Jesus then, again groaning within himself, came to the sepulchre. Now it was a cave, and a stone was laid over it. Jesus saith: take away the stone. Martha, the sister of him who was dead, saith to him: Lord, by this time his odor is offensive, for he is now four days dead. Jesus saith to her: did I not say to thee, that if thou believest, thou shalt see the glory of God? Then they took away the stone, and Jèsus lifting up his eyes, said: Father, I give thee thanks that thou hast heard me. I knew of a truth, that thou hearest me always; but I have spoken for the sake of the people who are around, that they may believe that thou hast sent me. When he had thus spoken, he cried with a loud voice: Lazarus, come forth! And immediately he that had been dead came forth, bound feet and hands with winding-bands, and his face bound about with a napkin. Jesus said to them: loose him and let him go.

Many, therefore, of the Jews who had come to Mary and Martha, and had seen what Jesus did, believed in him. But some of them went to the Pharisees and told them what Jesus had done. The chief priests, therefore, and Pharisees gathered a council, and they said: what do we? for this man worketh many miracles. If we let him thus alone, all will believe in him; and the Romans will come, and will take away our place and nation. But one among them, Caiphas by name, he being the high-priest for that year, said to them: ye know nothing at all, neither do ye consider, that it is expedient for you, that one man should die for the people, and that the whole nation perish not. Now this he said not of himself, but whereas he was the high-priest of that year, he prophesied that Jesus should die for the nation. And it

Whatsoever ye shall bind on earth shall be bound in heaven; and whatsoever ye shall loose on earth shall be loosed in heaven.—*St. Matthew xviii, 18.*

was not for the nation alone, but that he might gather together in one those children of God that are scattered abroad.

So, from that day forward, they took counsel together that they might put him to death.

Wherefore, Jesus walked no more openly among the Jews; but he departed into the country near the desert, to a village that is called Ephraim, and there he abode with his disciples.

And the Passover of the Jews was at hand; and many from the country went up to Jerusalem before the Passover, to purify themselves. They sought therefore for Jesus, and discoursed together, standing in the temple: what think ye, that he cometh not to the feast? And the chief-priests and Pharisees had given a commandment, that if any one knew where he was, he should tell it, that they might lay hold upon him.

Then Jesus, six days before the Passover, came to Bethany, where Lazarus had died, whom Jesus raised to life. And they made him a supper there, and Martha served; but Lazarus was one of those that reclined at table with him. Then Mary took a pound of balsam of spikenard, very precious, and anointed the feet of Jesus, and wiped his feet with her hair; and the house was filled with the odor of the balsam. Thereupon said one of his disciples, Judas Iscariot, who was about to betray him: why was not this balsam sold for three hundred denarii and given to the poor? And this he said, not because he cared for the poor, but because he was a thief, and having the money-casket, took away what was put therein. Jesus said, therefore: let her alone, that she may keep that for the day of my burial. For the poor ye have always with you, but me ye have not always.

A great multitude, therefore, of the Jews knew that he was there, and they came, not only on account of Jesus, but also that they might see Lazarus whom he had raised from the dead. But the princes of the priests were minded to kill Lazarus also, because many of the Jews, by reason of him, went away from them and believed in Jesus.

And, on the morrow, a great multitude who had come up to the festival day, when they had heard that Jesus was coming to Jerusalem, took branches of palm-trees, and went forth to meet him, and they shouted aloud: blessed be he who cometh in the name of the Lord, even the King of Israel. And Jesus found a young ass, and sat upon it, as it is written: fear not, daughter of Sion: behold, thy king cometh to thee, sitting upon an ass's colt. These things understood not his disciples at first; but when Jesus was glorified, then they remembered that these things had been written of him, and that they had done these things unto him. Many of the people who had been with him when he called Lazarus out of his grave, and raised him from the dead, gave their testimony accordingly; and for this reason, the multitude who had heard that he wrought this miracle came also out to meet him. Therefore, the Pharisees said among themselves: do ye see that we prevail nothing? behold all the world hath gone after him.

Now there were some gentiles among those who came up to adore on the festival day. These, therefore, approached unto Philip, who was of Bethsaida in Galilee, and made a request of him, saying: sir, we wish to see Jesus. Philip cometh and telleth Andrew: again Andrew and Philip told Jesus. But Jesus answered them, saying: the hour hath come that the Son of Man should be glorified. Verily, verily, I say unto you: unless the grain of wheat falling into the ground die, itself remaineth alone; but if it die, it bringeth forth much fruit. He who loveth his own life shall lose it; and he that hateth his life in this world, keepeth it unto life eternal. If any man serve me, let him follow me; and where I am, there shall also my servant be. If any man hath served me, him will my Father honor. Now is my soul troubled. And what shall I say? Father, save me from this hour? But for this cause came I unto this hour. Father, glorify thy name. A voice, therefore, came out of heaven: I have hitherto glorified it, and I will glorify it again. The crowd, therefore, who were standing about, when they heard the sound, said that it was thunder; but some others said that an angel had spoken to him. Jesus answered and said: the voice came not for my sake, but in behalf of yourselves. Now is the judgment of the world; now the prince of this world shall be cast out. And I, if I shall be lifted up from the earth, will draw all things to myself. (And this he said, signifying by what death he was about to die.) The multitude answered him: we have heard from the law that the Christ remaineth for ever: and how sayest thou that the Son of Man must be lifted up? Who is this Son of Man? Jesus therefore said to them: yet a little while is the light in you. Walk, while ye have light, that the shades of darkness do not encompass you. For he who walketh in the dark knoweth not whither he is going. While ye have light believe in the light, that ye may be children of light.

These things spake Jesus; and he departed and hid himself from them.

But although he had wrought such great miracles before them, they did not believe in him: that the saying of the prophet Isaiah might be fulfilled, which he spake: Lord, who hath believed our report? And to whom hath the arm of the Lord been revealed? Wherefore they could not believe, because Isaiah said again: he hath blinded their eyes, and hardened their heart, that they should not see with their eyes, nor understand with their heart, and be converted, and I should heal them. These things said Isaiah, when he saw his glory and spake of him. However, even of the chief men, many did believe in him; but on account of the Pharisees they did not confess it, that they might not be cast out of the synagogue. For they loved the glory of men more than the glory of God.

And Jesus cried aloud and said: he that believeth in me, believeth not in me, but in him that sent me. And he that seeth me, seeth him that sent me. I am come a light

And having taken the chalice, he gave thanks, and said, Take, and divide it among you.—*St. Luke xxii. 17.*

into the world, that every one who believeth in me, may not remain in darkness. And if any one hear my words and keepeth them not, I do not judge him, for I am not come to judge the world, but to save the world. Whoso despiseth me and doth not receive my words, hath that which will judge him; even the word which I have spoken. That will judge him on the last day. For I have not spoken of myself, but he that sent me, the Father, he himself gave me commandment what I should say and what I should speak. And I know that his commandment is eternal life. The things, therefore, that I speak, as the Father said to me, so I speak.

Before the festival day of the Passover, Jesus knowing that his hour was come, that he should pass out of the world to the Father; having loved his own who were in the world, he loved them unto the end. And during supper, (the devil having now put into the heart of Judas Iscariot the son of Simon to betray him,) knowing that the Father had given all things into his hands, and that he came from God, and goeth to God, he riseth from supper, and layeth aside his outer garments, and having taken a towel, he girded himself therewith. After that he poureth water into a basin, and began to wash the feet of his disciples, and to wipe them with the towel wherewith he was girded. He cometh, therefore, to Simon Peter. And Peter saith to him: Lord, dost thou wash my feet? Jesus answered and said unto him: what I am doing thou knowest not now, but thou shalt know hereafter. Peter saith to him: thou shalt never wash my feet. Jesus answered him: if I wash thee not, thou shalt have no part with me. Simon Peter saith to him: Lord, not my feet only, but my hands also, and my head. Jesus saith to him: he that is washed, needeth only to wash his feet, but is wholly clean. And ye are clean, but not all. For he knew who was the one who would betray him: wherefore he said: ye are not all clean. Then, after that he had washed their feet, and had taken his garments, when he had reclined again, he said to them: know ye what I have done to you? Ye call me the Teacher, and the Lord; and ye say well, for so I am. If then I, the Lord and the Teacher, have washed your feet; ye also ought to wash the feet of each other. For I have given you an example, that in like manner as I have done to you, so ye also may do. Verily, verily, I say unto you: the servant is not greater than his lord, nor the messenger greater than him that sent him. If ye know these things, blessed will ye be if ye do them. I speak not of all of you: I know whom I have chosen; but that the Scripture may be fulfilled, he that eateth my bread shall lift up his heel against me. I tell you now, before it come to pass, that when it shall have come to pass ye may believe that I Am. Verily, verily, I say unto you: he that receiveth whomsoever I shall send, receiveth me; and he that receiveth me, receiveth him that sent me. When Jesus had said these things, he was troubled in spirit, and he testified and said:

verily, verily, I say unto you: that one of you shall betray me. The disciples, therefore, looked at one another, doubting of whom he spake. Now there was leaning on the bosom of Jesus one of his disciples whom Jesus loved. Simon Peter, therefore, beckoned to him, and said to him: who is it of whom he speaketh? He, therefore, leaning back on the breast of Jesus, saith to him: Lord, who is it? Jesus answered: it is he to whom I will give some dipped bread. And when he had dipped a piece of bread, he gave it to Judas Iscariot, Simon's son. And after the morsel, Satan entered into him. And Jesus said to him: what thou doest, do quickly. Now no one of those who were at the table knew for what purpose he said this to him. For some thought, because Judas had the purse, that Jesus had said to him: buy those things which we have need of for the feast; or that he should give something to the poor. He then, when he had received the morsel, went immediately out. And it was night.

When therefore he was gone out, Jesus said: now is the Son of Man glorified, and God is glorified in him. If God be glorified in him, God also will glorify him in himself, and straightway will he glorify him. Little children, yet a little while I am with you. Ye shall seek me, and as I said to the Jews, whither I go ye cannot come, I say it now to you. A new commandment I give you: that ye love one another; as I have loved you, that ye love one another.

By this shall all men know that ye are my disciples, if ye have love one for another. Simon Peter saith to him: Lord, whither goest thou? Jesus answered: whither I go thou canst not follow me now; but thou shalt follow afterwards. Peter saith to him: why cannot I follow thee now? I will lay down my life for thee. Jesus answered him: wilt thou lay down thy life for me? Verily, verily, I say to thee, the cock shall not crow, until thou thrice deny me.

Let not your heart be troubled. Ye believe in God; believe also in me. In my

Father's house are many mansions. If it were not so, I would have said to you, that I go to prepare for you a place. And if I go and prepare a place for you, I am coming again, and I will receive you to myself, that where I am, ye also may be. And whither I go ye know, and the way ye know. Thomas saith to him: Lord, we know not whither thou goest, and how can we know the way? Jesus saith to him: I am the way, and the truth, and the life. No one cometh to the Father except through me. If ye had known me, of a truth ye would also have known my Father, and from henceforth ye will know him, and ye have seen him. Philip saith to him: Lord, show us the Father, and it is enough for us. Jesus saith to him: so long a time I am with you, and ye have not known me? Philip, he who seeth me, seeth also the Father. How sayest thou then: show us the Father? Do ye not believe that I am in the Father, and the Father is in me? The words that I speak to you, I speak not of myself. But the Father, abiding in me, he

Sleepest thou? Couldst thou not watch one hour?—*St. Mark xiv. 37.*

doeth the works. Do ye not believe that I am in the Father, and the Father is in me? Otherwise, believe on account of the works themselves. Verily, verily, I say unto you: whoso believeth in me, the works which I do, he also will do; and greater than these will he do, because I go to the Father. And whatsoever ye shall ask of the Father, in my name, that I will do, that the Father may be glorified in the Son. If ye shall ask anything of me, in my name, that I will do. If ye love me, keep my commandments. And I will ask the Father, and he will give you another Paraclete, that he may abide with you for ever, the Spirit of Truth, whom the world cannot receive, because it seeth him not, neither knoweth him; but ye shall know him, because he shall abide with you, and will be in you. I will not leave you orphans: I will come to you. Yet a little while, and the world seeth me no longer. But ye shall see me, because I live and ye shall live. In that day ye will know that I am in my Father, and ye in me, and I in you. Whoso hath my commandments, and keepeth them, he it is that loveth me. And he that loveth me will be loved of my Father. And I will live in him, and will manifest myself to him. Judas, not the Iscariot, saith to him: Lord, what hath come to pass, that thou art about to manifest thyself unto us, and not unto the world? Jesus answered and said unto him: if any one loveth me, he will keep my word, and my Father will love him and we will come unto him, and will make our abode with him. He who loveth me not, keepeth not my words. And the word which ye have heard is not mine, but his who sent me, even the Father. I have spoken these things to you, while remaining with you. But the Paraclete, the Holy Spirit, whom the Father will send in my name, he will teach you all things, and will remind you of all things whatsoever I have said to you. Peace I leave with you, my peace I give unto you; not as the world giveth give I unto you. Let not your heart be troubled, neither let it be afraid. Ye have heard that I said to you: I go, and I come to you. If ye loved me, ye would surely be glad, because I said I go to the Father, forasmuch as the Father is greater than I. And now I have told you, before it come to pass, that when it shall come to pass ye may believe. I will no more speak many things with you: for the prince of this world cometh, and in me he hath not anything. But I do in such wise that the world may know that I love the Father, even accordingly, as the Father hath given to me a commandment. Arise, let us go hence.

I am the true vine, and my Father is the husbandman. Every branch in me not bearing fruit he will lop it off; and every one bearing fruit, he will prune it, that it may bear more fruit. Now ye are clean, by reason of the word which I have spoken to you. Abide in me, and I in you. As a branch cannot bear fruit of itself, or unless it abide in the vine; so neither can ye, unless ye abide in me. I am the vine, ye are the branches; he that abideth in me and I in him, the same beareth much fruit, for apart from me ye can do nothing. If any one abide not in me, he will be lopped off like the branch which withereth, and they will gather it up, and cast it into the fire, and it is burnt up.

If ye shall remain in me, and my words shall remain in you, ye may ask whatsoever ye will, and it shall be done for you. In this is my Father glorified, that ye bear very much fruit, and become my disciples. As my Father hath loved me, I have likewise loved you. Abide in my love. If ye keep my commandments, ye will remain in my love; as I, likewise, have kept my Father's commandments, and I remain in his love. These things have I spoken unto you, that your joy may be in you, and that your joy may become full. This is my commandment: that ye love one another, in like manner as I have loved you. Greater love than this hath no man: that a man lay down his life for his friends. Ye are my friends, if ye do the things that I command you. I will no more call you bond-servants, for the bond-servant knoweth not what his lord doeth: but I have named you friends; because all things whatsoever I have heard of my Father, I have made known unto you. Ye have not chosen me; but I have chosen you, and I have appointed you, that ye may go forth, and may bring forth fruit, and your fruit may remain, so that whatsoever ye ask the Father in my name, he may give it you. These things I prescribe unto you, so that ye may love one another. If the world hate you, know ye that it hath held me in hatred before you. If ye had been of the world, the world would love what was its own: but because ye are not of the world, inasmuch as I have chosen you out of the world, for this reason the world hated you. Bear in mind my word which I spake to you: the servant is not greater than his lord. If they have persecuted me, they will also persecute you; if they have kept my word, they will keep yours also. But all these things will they do to you, for my name's sake, because they know not him that sent me. If I had not come and spoken to them, they would not have any sin: but now they have no excuse for their sin. Whoso hateth me, hateth also my Father. If I had not done works among them such as no other man ever did, they would not have any sin; but now they have both seen and hated both me and my Father. But this is so, that the word may be fulfilled which is written in their law: for they have hated me without any cause. But when the Paraclete cometh, whom I will send to you from the Father, the Spirit of Truth who proceedeth from the Father, he will bear witness concerning me. And ye shall bear witness, because ye are with me from the beginning.

I have spoken these things to you, that ye may not be made to stumble. They will put you out of the synagogues; moreover, the hour cometh when every one who killeth you will think that he offereth homage to God.

And these things will they do to you, because they have neither known my Father nor me. But I have told these things to

And the Lord turned and looked upon Peter. And Peter remembered the word.
—*St. Luke xxii. 61.*

you, that when their hour cometh, ye may call to mind that I told you of them. Now, I did not tell you of these things from the beginning, because I was with you; but presently I am going unto him that sent me; yet no one of you asketh me, whither goest thou? But because I have said these things to you, sorrow hath filled your heart. Nevertheless, I tell you the truth; it is for your advantage that I go away, for if I do not depart from you, the Paraclete will not come to you; but if I do go away, I will send him to you. And he, when he is come, will convict the world, in respect of sin, and of righteousness, and of judgment. In respect of sin, truly, because they have not believed in me; in respect of righteousness, moreover, because I go to the Father, and ye will see me no more; and also in respect of judgment, because the prince of this world is already judged.

Many things besides have I to say to you, but ye cannot bear them now. Howbeit, when he, the Spirit of Truth, is come, he will teach you all truth: for he will not speak from himself, but whatsoever things he shall hear he will speak, and he will show to you the things that are to come. He will glorify me, because he will take of mine, and will show it to you. All things whatsoever that the Father hath are mine. For this reason I said: that he will receive of mine and show it to you. A little while and ye behold me no more, and again a little while and ye shall see me, because I go to the Father. Then some of his disciples said one to another: what is this that he saith to us: a little while and ye behold me not, and again a little while and ye shall see me; and because I go to the Father? They said, therefore, what is it that he is speaking about; a little while? We do not understand what he is saying. And Jesus knew that they were wishing to question him, and he said to them: do ye inquire among yourselves concerning this, that I said a little while and ye will not see me, and again a little while and ye will see me? Verily, verily, I say unto you, that ye shall lament and weep, while the world will rejoice; and ye shall be made sorrowful, but your sorrow will be turned into joy. A woman when she is in travail hath sorrow because her hour is come; but when she hath brought forth the child, she remembereth no more the anguish for joy that a man is born into the world. And ye, likewise, at present, have indeed sorrow, but I will see you again, and your heart will be gladdened, and your joy no man will take away from you. And in that day, ye will not have to ask me anything.

Verily, verily, I say unto you: if ye shall make any petition to the Father in my name, he will give it you. Hitherto, ye have not asked for anything in my name. Ask, and ye will receive, so that your joy may become full. I have spoken these things to you as parables. The hour cometh wherein I will no longer speak to you in parables, but will plainly declare to you concerning the Father. In that day ye shall make petitions in my name, and I say not to you, that I will make request of the Father in your behalf: for the Father himself loveth you, because you have loved me, and believed that I came forth from God. I went forth from the Father, and I am come into the world; again, I leave the world, and I am going to the Father.

His disciples say to him: lo, now thou speakest openly, and thou sayest no parable. Now we perceive that thou knowest all things, and needest not that any man question thee; by this we believe, that thou camest forth from God. Jesus answered them: do ye now believe? Behold the hour cometh, yea, is at hand, when ye will be scattered, each one to his own place, and will leave me alone; and yet I am not alone, for the Father is with me. I have said these things to you, that ye may have peace in me. In the world ye will have distress: but take courage; I have overcome the world.

These things spake Jesus, and lifting up his eyes to heaven, he said: Father, the hour is come; glorify thy Son, that thy Son may glorify thee; as thou hast given him power over all flesh, that all whatsoever thou hast given him, to them he may give eternal life. And this is the eternal life, that they may know thee the only true God, and him whom thou didst send, even Jesus Christ. I have glorified thee on the earth: I have finished the work which thou gavest me to do. And now, glorify thou me, O Father, with thyself, with the glory which I had with thee before the world was. I have manifested thy name to the men whom thou hast given me out of the world. Thine they were, and thou gavest them to me; and they have kept thy word. Now they have known that all things which thou hast given me are from thee; because the words which thou hast given me I have given unto them, and they have received them, and have known of a truth that I came forth from thee, and they believed that thou didst send me. For these I pray; not for the world do I pray, but for those whom thou hast given me, for thine they are. And all things that are mine are thine, and thine are mine, and in them am I glorified. And now I am no more in the world, and they are in the world, and I come to thee. Holy Father, keep in thy name those whom thou hast given me, that they may be one, in like manner as we are. While I was with them, I kept them in thy name. Those whom thou gavest me I have guarded, and not one of them perished, but the son of perdition, that the Scripture might be fulfilled. And now I come to thee, and these things I say in the world, that they may have in themselves the fulness of my joy. I have given unto them thy word, and the world hath had them in hatred, because they are not of the world, even as I am not of the world. I pray not that thou take them out of the world, but that thou keep them from evil. They are not of the world; consecrate them in the truth. Thy word is truth. As thou hast sent me into the world, even so have I sent them into the world. And for their sakes I consecrate myself, that they also may be themselves consecrated in truth. And not for them only do I pray, but for those also who will hereafter believe in me through

His blood be on us, and on our children.—*St. Matthew xxvii. 25.*

their word; that they may be all one, as thou Father in me and I in thee, that they also may be one in us, that the world may believe that thou didst send me. And the glory which thou gavest to me, I have given to them, that they may be one in like manner as we are one. I in them, and thou in me, that they may be perfected into one, and the world may know that thou didst send me, and hast loved them even as thou hast loved me. Father, I will that where I am, they also whom thou hast given me, may be with me; that they may behold my glory which thou gavest me, for thou lovedst me before the foundation of the world. Just Father, the world knew thee not; but I did know thee, and these knew that thou didst send me. And I made known to them thy name, and I will make it known, that the love wherewith thou lovedst me may be in them, and I in them.

When Jesus had spoken these words he went forth with his disciples over the brook

Kidron, where was a garden, into which he entered, himself and his disciples. And Judas also, who betrayed him, knew the place; for Jesus had ofttimes resorted thither together with his disciples. Judas, then, having received a cohort with officers, from the chief-priests and Pharisees, cometh thither, with lanterns, and torches, and weapons. Jesus, therefore, knowing all things which were to befall him, went forward, and said to them: whom seek ye? They answered him: Jesus of Nazareth. Jesus saith to them: I am he. And Judas, also, who betrayed him, was standing with them. When, therefore, he said to them: I am he; they went backward, and fell to the ground. Then he asked them once more: whom seek ye? And they said: Jesus of Nazareth. Jesus answered: I have told you that I am he; if therefore ye seek me, let these go their way; that the word might be fulfilled which he spake: of those whom thou gavest me, I lost not one. Then Simon Peter, having a sword, drew it, and struck the servant of the high-priest, and cut off his right ear. Now the servant's name was Malchus. Then Jesus said to Peter: Put up thy sword into the sheath. The cup which my Father hath given me, shall I not drink it? Whereupon the cohort, and the tribune, and the officers of the Jews seized hold of Jesus, and bound him, and they led him away first to Annas; for he was father-in-law to Caiphas, who was the high-priest of that year. Now Caiphas was he that had given counsel to the Jews: that it was expedient that one man should die for the people. Now Simon Peter was following after Jesus, and likewise another disciple. And that disciple was known to the high-priest, and he entered in with Jesus into the court of the high-priest; but Peter was standing at the door without. So then, that disciple who was known to the high-priest went out, and spoke to her who kept the door, and brought in Peter. The maid who kept the door saith therefore to Peter: art thou not also one of the disciples of this man? He saith: I am not. Now the servants and the officers were standing by a fire of coals, for it was cold, and were warming themselves, and Peter also was standing among them, and was warming himself.

The high-priest, accordingly, questioned Jesus concerning his disciples, and concerning his teaching. Jesus answered him: I have spoken openly to the world; I have ever taught in the synagogue and in the temple, where all the Jews are wont to assemble, and in secret I have spoken nothing. Wherefore dost thou question me? question them that have heard me as to what I have spoken to themselves: behold, these know what things I have said. And when he had said these things, one of the officers standing by gave Jesus a slap with the hand, saying: answerest thou thus to the high-priest? Jesus answered him: if I have spoken ill, bear witness of the evil; but if well, why smitest thou me?

And Annas sent him bound to the high-priest Caiphas.

Now Peter was standing and warming himself. They said therefore unto him: art

Daughters of Jerusalem, weep not for me, but weep for yourselves, and for your children.—*St. Luke xxiii. 28.*

not thou also of his disciples? He denied it, and he said: I am not. One of the high-priest's servants, a kinsman of the one whose ear Peter cut off, saith to him: did not I see thee with him in the garden? Then Peter again denied; and immediately the cock crew.

Then they led forth Jesus from Caiphas to the pretorium. And it was early morning; and they went not themselves into the pretorium, that they might not be defiled, but might eat the passover. Pilate therefore went forth to them without, and he saith to them: what accusation bring ye against this man? They answered and said unto him: if he were not an evil-doer, we would not have delivered him over unto thee. Then Pilate said to them: do ye take him, and according to your law, execute sentence upon him. The Jews therefore said to him: it is not lawful for us to put any man to death. That the word of Jesus might be fulfilled, signifying by what death he should die. Pilate, accordingly, went in again, into the pretorium, and he called Jesus and said to him: art thou the King of the Jews? Jesus answered: sayest thou this, of thyself, or did others say it to thee of me? Pilate answered: am I indeed a Jew? Thine own nation and the chief-priests have delivered thee over to me: what hast thou done? Jesus answered: my kingdom is not of this world; if my kingdom were of this world, my servants would certainly strive, that I might not be delivered up to the Jews; but now is my kingdom not from hence. Pilate therefore said to him: art thou a king then? Jesus answered: thou sayest that I am a king.* For this was I born, and for this came I into the world, that I should bear witness to the truth. Every one who is of the truth, heareth my voice. Pilate saith to him: what is truth? And when he had said this, he went out again to the Jews, and he saith to them: I find in him no guilt. But ye have a custom that I should release one to you, at the Passover. Will

---

* The sense is: thou sayest, truly, that I am a king.

ye, therefore, that I release to you the king of the Jews? Then they all cried out again, saying: not this man but Barabbas. Now, Barabbas was a robber.

Then, accordingly, Pilate had Jesus seized and scourged. And the soldiers plaiting a crown out of thorns placed it on his head, and they put around him a purple garment. And they came up to him, and they said: hail, king of the Jews! and they gave him blows. And Pilate went out again and he saith to them: behold, I bring him forth to you, that ye may know that I find no guilt in him. (Jesus, accordingly, came out, wearing the crown of thorns, and the purple garment.) And he saith to them: behold the man! When therefore the chief-priests and officers had seen him, they cried out: crucify, crucify him! Pilate saith to them: do ye take him and crucify him; for I find in him no guilt. The Jews answered him: we have a law, and according to the law, he ought to die: because he made himself out to be the Son of God. When therefore Pilate had heard this saying, he was the more afraid. And he went again into the pretorium, and said to Jesus: whence art thou? But Jesus gave him no answer. Pilate thereupon saith to him: speakest thou not to me? knowest thou not that I have power to crucify thee, and have power to release thee? Jesus answered: thou wouldst not have any power against me, unless it had been given thee from above. Therefore, he that delivered me unto thee hath greater sin. Upon this, Pilate sought to release him; but the Jews cried out: if thou release this man, thou art not a friend of Cæsar, for every man who maketh himself out a king, opposeth Cæsar. Now when Pilate had heard these words, he brought Jesus out, and sat down on the judgment seat, in a place called the Pavement, and in Hebrew Gabbatha. And it was the preparation of the Passover, about the sixth hour, and he saith to the Jews: behold your King! But they cried out: away with him, away with him, crucify him! Pilate saith to them: shall I crucify your King? The chief-priests answered: we have

Father, into thy hands I commend my spirit.—*St. Luke xxiii. 46.*

no king but Cæsar. And thereupon he delivered him unto them, to be crucified.

So, they took Jesus, and led him away. And bearing the cross for himself, he went forth to that place which is called Calvary, and in Hebrew Golgotha, where they crucified him, and two others with him, on either side one, and Jesus in the midst. And Pilate wrote also a title and put it on the cross. And the writing was JESUS OF NAZARETH, THE KING OF THE JEWS. This title, therefore, many of the Jews read, because the place where Jesus was crucified was nigh to the city; and it was written in Hebrew, and in Greek; and in Latin. Then the chief-priests of the Jews said to Pilate: write not, the King of the Jews, but that he said, I am the King of the Jews. Pilate answered: what I have written, I have written. The soldiers, therefore, when they had crucified him, took his garments, and they made four parts, to every soldier a part, and his tunic. Now the tunic was without seam, woven from the top throughout. They said therefore among themselves, let us not cut it, but let us cast lots for it, whose it shall be ; that the Scripture might be fulfilled, saying: they have parted my garments among them, and on my vesture they have cast lots. And the soldiers accordingly did these things.

. Now, there stood by the cross of Jesus, his mother, and Mary his mother's sister, the wife of Cleophas, and Mary Magdalen. When, therefore, Jesus saw his mother and the disciple whom he loved, standing near by, he saith to his mother: woman, behold thy son. Then he saith to the disciple: behold thy mother. And from that hour the disciple took her unto his own house.

Afterwards, Jesus knowing that all things were accomplished ; that the Scripture might be fulfilled, said: I thirst. Now there was a vessel set there full of vinegar. And they, putting a sponge soaked in the vinegar upon hyssop, brought it to his mouth. When, therefore, Jesus had received the vinegar, he said: it is finished,

And bowing down his head, he gave up the ghost.

Then the Jews, (because it was the Preparation,) that the bodies might not remain upon the cross on the sabbath, (for that sabbath day was a high day,) besought Pilate that their legs might be broken, and that they might be taken away. Accordingly, the soldiers came, and they did, indeed, break the legs of the first, and of the other who was crucified with Jesus; but when they came to Jesus, as they perceived him to be already dead, they did not break his legs. Howbeit, one of the soldiers with a spear pierced his side, and straightway there came out blood and water. And he who hath seen hath borne witness, and his witness is true, and he knoweth that he saith the truth, that ye also may believe. For these things came to pass, that the Scripture might be fulfilled: ye shall not break a bone of him. And again another Scripture saith: they shall look on him whom they pierced.

And after these things, Joseph of Arimathea, because he was a disciple of Jesus; though a concealed one, on account of his fear of the Jews; besought Pilate that he might take away the body of Jesus. And Pilate gave leave. So then he came and took away the body of Jesus. And there came also Nicodemus, the same who at the first had come to Jesus by night, bringing a mixture of myrrh and aloes, about a hundred pound weight. They took the body of Jesus, accordingly, and wrapped it closely in linen cloths together with the spices, as the custom of Jews is to bury. Now there was in the place where he was crucified a garden, and in the garden a new sepulchre, wherein no one had yet been laid. Therein, because of the Day of Preparation of the Jews, and for that the sepulchre was nigh at hand, they accordingly laid Jesus.

Now, on the first day of the week, Mary Magdalen cometh early, while it was yet dark, to the sepulchre, and seeth the stone taken away from the sepulchre. She ran

In the garden was a new sepulchre, wherein was never man yet laid.
—*St. John xix. 41.*

therefore, and came to Simon Peter and the other disciple whom Jesus loved, and she saith to them: they have taken away the Lord from the sepulchre, and we know not where they have laid him. Peter therefore went out, and that other disciple, and they came to the sepulchre. Now they were both running together, and that other disciple ran before, more quickly than Peter, and came first to the sepulchre. And when he stooped down, he saw the linen cloths lying; but he did not go in. Then came Simon Peter, following him, and he went in, and he saw the linen cloths lying, and the napkin which had been about his head, not lying with the linen cloths, but folded up separately in a place apart. Then, that other disciple who had come first to the sepulchre also went in, and he believed. For, until then, they understood not the Scripture, that it behooved him to rise from the dead. Then the disciples returned again to their own place.

But Mary stayed without, by the sepulchre, weeping. And, while she was weeping, she stooped down and looked into the sepulchre, and she saw two angels in white, sitting, one at the head, another at the feet, where the body of Jesus had been laid. They say to her: woman, why weepest thou? She saith to them: because they have taken away my Lord, and I know not where they have laid him. When she had thus said, she turned around, and saw Jesus standing, and knew not that it was Jesus. Jesus saith to her: woman, why weepest thou? whom art thou seeking? She, thinking it was the gardener, saith to him: sir, if thou hast taken him hence, tell me where thou hast laid him, and I will take him away. Jesus saith to her: Mary! She, turning, saith to him, Rabboni! (that is to say, Master.) Jesus saith to her: embrace me not; for I am not yet ascended to my Father: but go to my brethren, and say to them: I ascend to my Father and your Father, my God and your God. Mary Magdalen cometh, telling the disciples: I have seen the Lord, and these things said he to me.

Then, when it was evening, on that same day, the first of the week, and the doors were fast closed where the disciples were gathered, for fear of the Jews, came Jesus and stood in the midst, and saith unto them: peace be unto you! And when he had said this, he showed unto them his hands and his side. The disciples, therefore, rejoiced at seeing the Lord. Then he said to them again: peace be unto you; as my Father sent me, I also send you. When he had thus said, he breathed on them, and he said unto them: receive ye the Holy Ghost: whosoever sins ye shall forgive, they are forgiven unto them; and whosoever ye shall retain, they are retained.

Now, Thomas, who is called The Twin, was not with them when Jesus came. The other disciples said, therefore, unto him: we have seen the Lord. But he said unto them: unless I shall see in his hands the print of the nails, and put my finger into the place of the nails, and put my hand into his side, I will not believe. And after eight days, the disciples were again within, and Thomas with them. Jesus cometh, the doors being shut, and he stood in the midst, and he said : peace unto you. Then saith he to Thomas : reach hither thy finger and feel my hands, and reach hither thy hand and put it into my side, and be not faithless but believing. Thomas answered and said unto him : my Lord, and my God! Jesus said unto him : because thou hast seen me, Thomas, thou hast believed. Blessed are they who have not seen, and have believed.

Many truly, and other signs, also, wrought Jesus, in the presence of his disciples, which are not written in this book. But these are written, that ye may believe that Jesus is the Christ, the Son of God, and that, believing, ye may have life in his name.

Afterwards, Jesus manifested himself again to his disciples, at the sea of Tiberias. And he made the manifestation after this wise.

There were together, Simon Peter, and

Jesus saith unto her, Woman, why weepest thou?—*St. John xx. 15.*

Thomas who is called The Twin, and Nathanael who was from Cana of Galilee, and the sons of Zebedee, and two others of his disciples. Simon Peter saith to them: I go a fishing. They say to him: we also come with thee. And they went forth and entered into the vessel; and that night they took nothing. And when the morning dawned, Jesus stood on the shore; the disciples, however, knew not that it was Jesus. Then Jesus said to them: children, have ye aught to eat? They answered him: no. He saith to them: cast the net on the right side of the vessel, and ye will find. Then they cast it; and now they were not able to draw it, for the multitude of the fishes. Upon this, that disciple whom Jesus loved said to Peter: it is the Lord. Simon Peter, when he heard that it was the Lord, girt himself about with his tunic, (for he was stripped of his outer garment,) and cast himself into the sea. And the other disciples came in the vessel, (for they were not far from land, only about two hundred cubits,) and they were dragging the net of fishes.

As soon, then, as they had landed, they saw a fire of coals prepared, and a fish laid thereon, and bread. Jesus saith to them: bring some of the fishes ye have just taken. Simon Peter therefore went aboard, and drew the net to land, full of large fishes, a hundred and fifty-three; and for all there were so many, the net was not torn. Jesus saith to them: come, and break your fast. And none of them who were sitting at the meal durst ask him, who art thou? knowing that it was the Lord. And Jesus cometh, and taketh bread and giveth to them, and likewise fish.

And thus, for the third time, was Jesus manifested to his disciples, after he had risen from the dead.

When, therefore, they had finished their meal, Jesus saith to Simon Peter: Simon, son of John, lovest thou me more than these? He saith to him: yea, Lord, thou knowest that I love thee. He saith to him: feed my lambs. He saith to him, again: Simon, son of John, lovest thou me? He saith to him: yea, Lord, thou knowest that

I love thee. He saith to him: feed my lambs. He saith to him the third time: Simon, son of John, lovest thou me? Peter was grieved, because he said to him the third time, lovest thou me? and he said to him: Lord, thou knowest all things: thou knowest that I love thee. He said to him: be the shepherd of my sheep.

Verily, verily, I say unto thee: when thou wast younger, thou didst gird thyself, and didst walk whither thou wouldst. But when thou art old, thou wilt stretch forth thy hands, and another will gird thee, and lead thee whither thou wouldst not. And this he said, signifying by what death he should glorify God. And having said this, he saith to him: follow me. Peter turning round, saw that disciple whom Jesus loved following, who also leaned on his breast at supper, and said: Lord, who is it that will betray thee? When, therefore, Peter had looked on him, he said to Jesus: Lord, but what of this man? Jesus saith to him: so I will have him remain till I come, what is it to thee? follow thou me. This saying, therefore, went abroad among the brethren, that that disciple should not die. And Jesus did not say to him, he should not die; but, so I will have him remain till I come, what is it to thee? This is that disciple who giveth testimony of these things, and who wrote these things: and we know that his testimony is true.

But there are, also, many other things which Jesus did: which, if they were written, every one, the world itself, I think, would not be able to contain the books that should be written.

But they constrained him, saying, Abide with us.—*St. Luke xxiv.* 29.

AN EPISTLE

OF

ST. JOHN THE APOSTLE

TO THE

SEVEN CHURCHES OF ASIA, CONVEYING MESSAGES FROM JESUS CHRIST TO THEIR BISHOPS.

THESE seven churches became metropolitan sees, with the exception of Thyatira, which lost its original pre-eminence in the second century. The Bishop of Ephesus was a superior metropolitan, or, in the later ecclesiastical language, an exarch. The Third Ecumenical Council was held in the cathedral of Ephesus, in the fifth century, under the presidency of St. Cyril of Alexandria as Papal legate, and condemned the Nestorian heresy. The Latrocinium, or Robber-Synod, was afterwards held in the same place, under Dioscorus, the successor of St. Cyril in the see of Alexandria, in the interest of the Eutychian heresy; which was condemned by the Fourth Ecumenical Council of Chalcedon. St. Timothy was the first Bishop of Ephesus, consecrated by St. Paul, who addressed to him two Pastoral Epistles. It is probable that his martyrdom had taken place before the Apocalypse was written, and that the Epistle to the Angel of Ephesus was addressed to his successor. St. Polycarp was the first Bishop of Smyrna, consecrated by St. John, and to him St. Ignatius addressed one of his Seven Epistles, written on his way to martyrdom at Rome. An archbishop of Ephesus in the eighth century was one of the first promoters of the Iconoclastic heresy under Leo the Isaurian. Mark of Ephesus was the principal opponent of the reunion of the Greeks to the Roman Church, at the Council of Florence and afterwards. The city of Ephesus has long been in ruins, and its ancient see has only a nominal existence. Whether or no the ecclesiastical organization of provinces was already formally constituted at the end of the first century, the seven churches addressed by the apostle were evidently the principal churches of that part of Asia, and the mother churches to which the lesser bishoprics were affiliated; so that virtually, here as well as elsewhere, the metropolitan system existed in at least a rudimental state, and in the beginning of its later development.

INTRODUCTORY EPISTLE

ADDRESSED TO ALL THE SEVEN CHURCHES.

John to the seven churches which are in Asia: grace be unto you and peace, from him who is, and who was, and who is to come; and from the seven spirits who are before his throne; and from Jesus Christ, who is the faithful witness, the first-begotten of the dead, and the prince of the kings of the earth. Unto him who hath loved us, and hath washed us from our sins in his own blood, (and he made us to be a kingdom, and to be priests unto his God and Father;) to him be glory and the dominion unto ages of ages. Amen. Behold, he cometh with clouds, and every eye shall see him, even they who pierced him. And all the tribes of the earth shall mourn over him: Even so. Amen. I am the Alpha and the Omega, beginning and end, saith the

While he blessed them, he was parted from them, and carried up into heaven.—*St. Luke xxiv. 51.*

Lord God, who is, and who was, and who is to come, the Almighty.

I John, your brother and companion in the tribulation, and in the kingdom and patience which are in Christ Jesus, was in the island that is called Patmos, for the word of God, and for the testimony of Jesus Christ. I was in the spirit on the Lord's Day, and heard behind me a great voice, as of a trumpet, saying: what thou seest write in a book, and send it unto the seven churches which are in Asia; unto Ephesus, and Smyrna, and Pergamus, and Thyatira, and Sardis, and Philadelphia, and Laodicea. And I turned to see the voice that spoke with me. And being turned, I saw seven golden candlesticks, and in the midst of the seven golden candlesticks, one like unto the Son of Man, clothed in a garment down to his feet, and girt about the breasts with a golden girdle. His head and hair were white, like white wool and like snow; and his eyes like a flame of fire, and his feet were like fine brass as it were in a glowing furnace, and his voice was as the sound of many waters. He held in his right hand seven stars, and from his mouth came forth a sharp two-edged sword; and his face was as when the sun shineth in his full strength. And when I had seen him I fell at his feet, as if I were dead. And he laid his right hand upon me, saying: fear not; I am the first and the last and the Living One: and I was dead, and behold I am alive for evermore, and I have the keys of death and of Hades. Write, therefore, what things thou hast seen, and what things are now, and what things must come to pass after these. This is the mystery of the seven stars which thou hast seen in my right hand, and the seven golden candlesticks: the seven stars are the angels of the seven churches; and the seven candlesticks are the seven churches.

MESSAGE TO THE BISHOP OF EPHESUS.

Unto the Angel of the church of Ephesus write: these things saith he that holdeth the seven stars in his right hand, who walketh in the midst of the seven golden candlesticks. I know thy works, and thy labor, and thy patience, and how thou canst not bear them that are evil, and thou hast tried those who say they are apostles and are not, and hast found them liars; and thou hast patience, and hast borne up for my name's sake, and hast not faltered. But I have this against thee, that thou hast left thy first love. Be mindful, therefore, whence thou hast fallen, and do penance, and do thy first works; or else I come to thee, and I will remove thy candlestick from its place, unless thou do penance. But thou hast this, that thou hast hated the deeds of the Nicolaitans, which I also hate. He that hath an ear, let him hear what the Spirit saith to the churches. To him who overcometh I will give to eat from the tree of life which is in the Paradise of my God.

MESSAGE TO THE BISHOP OF SMYRNA.

And to the Angel of the church of Smyrna write: these things saith the first and the last, who was dead and who liveth. I know thy tribulation and thy poverty, but thou art rich, and thou art blasphemed by those who say they are Jews, and are not, but are a synagogue of Satan. Fear none of those things which thou shalt suffer. Behold, the devil shall cast some of you into prison, that ye may be tried; and ye shall have tribulation ten days. Be thou faithful even unto death, and I will give thee the crown of life. He that hath an ear, let him hear what the Spirit saith to the churches. He that overcometh shall not be hurt by the second death.

THE ASSUMPTION OF THE BLESSED VIRGIN.

MESSAGE TO THE BISHOP OF PERGAMUS.

And to the Angel of the church in Pergamus write: these things saith he who hath the sharp two-edged sword. I know where thou dwellest, where the throne of Satan is. And thou holdest fast my name, and hast not denied my faith, even in those days in which Antipas was my faithful martyr, who was slain among you, where Satan dwelleth. But I have a few things against thee, because thou hast there some who hold the doctrine of Balaam, who taught Balak to put a stumbling-block before the children of Israel, by tempting them to eat meats offered to idols and to commit fornication. So, thou also hast some who hold the doctrine of the Nicolaitans. Thou, likewise, do penance. Or else I will come to thee quickly, and will fight against them with the sword of my mouth. He that hath an ear, let him hear what the Spirit saith to the churches. To him who overcometh I will give hidden manna, and I will give him a white stone, and on the stone a new name written, which no one knoweth save he who receiveth it.

MESSAGE TO THE BISHOP OF THYATIRA.

And to the Angel of the church of Thyatira write: these things saith the Son of God, who hath eyes like a flame of fire, and his feet are like fine brass. I have known thy works, and thy faith, and thy charity, and thy service, and thy patience, and thy last works which are more than the first. But I have a few things against thee, because thou sufferest the woman Jezebel, who calleth herself a prophetess, to teach, and to seduce my servants to commit fornication and to eat things sacrificed to idols. And I have given her space to do penance, but she will not repent of her fornication. Behold, I will cast her into a bed, and those who have committed adultery with her shall be in the greatest tribulation, unless they have done penance for their works. And I will kill her children with death, and all the churches shall know that I am he who searcheth hearts and reins; and I will give to each one of you according to his works. But I say to you and to the rest who are in Thyatira; as many as do not hold this doctrine, and who have not known the depths of Satan, as men say; I will not lay any other burden upon you. Nevertheless, that which you have hold fast until I come. And whosoever hath overcome, and hath kept my works even until the end, to him I will give power over the nations, and he shall rule them with a rod of iron; and they shall be shattered like a potter's vessel, as I also have received of my Father. And I will give to him the morning-star. He that hath an ear, let him hear what the Spirit saith to the churches.

MESSAGE TO THE BISHOP OF SARDIS.

And to the Angel of the church of Sardis write: these things saith he that hath the seven spirits of God, and the seven stars. I know thy works, that thou hast a name that thou livest, and art dead. Become watchful, and strengthen the things that remain and were like to die, for I find not thy works complete before my God. Keep in mind, therefore, how thou hast received and heard, and take heed to it, and do penance. If therefore thou shalt not watch, I will come upon thee as a thief, and thou shalt not know at what hour I will come upon thee. But thou hast a few names in Sardis that have not defiled their garments, and they shall walk with me in white, for they are worthy. He that overcometh, shall thus be clothed in white garments; and I will not blot his name out of the book of life, but I will confess his name before my Father, and before his angels. He that hath an ear, let him hear what the Spirit saith to the churches.

MESSAGE TO THE BISHOP OF PHILADELPHIA.

To the Angel of the church of Philadelphia write: these things saith he that is holy, he that is true, he that hath the key of David, he that openeth and no man shutteth, and shutteth and no man openeth. I know thy works. Behold, I have set before thee an open door, and no man can shut it, for thou hast a little strength, and hast kept my word, and hast not denied my name. Behold, I will make those of the synagogue of Satan, who say they are Jews, and are not, but do lie; behold, I will make them to come and worship before thy feet, and to know that I have loved thee. Because thou hast kept the word of my patience, I also will keep thee from the hour of trial, which is about to come upon the whole world to try those who dwell on the earth. Behold, I come quickly. Hold fast that which thou hast, that no other take thy crown. Whoso overcometh, I will make him a pillar in the temple of my

God, and he shall nevermore go out; and I will write upon him the name of my God, and the name of the city of my God, the new Jerusalem, which cometh down from heaven from my God, and my own new name. He who hath an ear, let him hear what the Spirit saith to the churches.

MESSAGE TO THE BISHOP OF LAODICEA.

And to the Angel of the church of Laodicea write: these things saith the Amen, the faithful and true witness, the beginning of the creation of God. I know thy works, that thou art neither cold nor hot; I would thou wert either cold or hot. Wherefore, since thou art lukewarm, and neither cold nor hot, I am about to vomit thee out of my mouth. Because thou sayest: I am rich and abounding in wealth, and have need of nothing; and knowest not that thou art miserable, and pitiable, and poor, and blind, and naked; I counsel thee to buy of me gold tried in the fire, that thou mayest become rich, and be clothed with white garments, so that the shame of thy nakedness do not appear; and that thou anoint thine eyes with eye-salve, that thou mayest see. As many as I love I rebuke and chasten; be zealous, therefore, and do penance. Behold, I stand at the door and knock. If any one hear my voice, and open the door, I will come in to him, and will sup with him, and he with me. To him who overcometh, I will give to sit with me on my throne; even as I have overcome, and have sat down with my Father upon his throne. He that hath an ear, let him hear what the Spirit saith to the churches.

www.ingramcontent.com/pod-product-compliance
Lightning Source LLC
Chambersburg PA
CBHW021815230426
43669CB00008B/756